to Erna,
sometimes God
brings people into my life
that find a special place
in my heart— you are
one of those!
with love,
Julie

JAN 25
2016

THE MEGILLAH
OF ESTHER

*"Revelation of That Which Is
Hidden"—A Parable*

Julianna Joy Klassen

WESTBOW
PRESS®
A DIVISION OF THOMAS NELSON
& ZONDERVAN

WestBow Press books may be ordered through booksellers or by contacting:

WestBow Press
A Division of Thomas Nelson & Zondervan
1663 Liberty Drive
Bloomington, IN 47403
www.westbowpress.com
1 (866) 928-1240

ISBN: 978-1-5127-1900-0 (sc)

Library of Congress Control Number: 2015918304

Print information available on the last page.

WestBow Press rev. date: 11/05/2015

"… He is like a man observing his natural face in a mirror, for he observes himself, goes away and immediately forgets what kind of man he was,"
~James 1:23, 24.

How much time do we spend in front of a mirror, and yet, as James says, we walk away and immediately forget what we look like.

While we recognize ourselves and others by facial features, we are more than our outer appearance. We are body, soul, and spirit, as Paul points out in I Thessalonians 5:23.

We daily use mirrors to check our image – is our hair out of place, is our shirt buttoned wrong, do we have a smudge on our cheek - but we do not have a mirror that reflects back to us the condition of our inner man. But … what if we do? What if God gave us a parable that we can hold up as a mirror and see ourselves as we have never seen ourselves before?

This book presents Esther as God's parable, or mirror, that reveals to us how we work and rule within our 'kingdom' – our soul and spirit residing in a physical body.

CONTENTS

INTRODUCTION

Do you love a mystery? Hidden meanings, double meanings? An intriguing story? History?

The book of Esther offers it all. It is a diamond mine of truth that is rarely excavated. Most people read it, see only the obvious storyline, and miss the depth of meaning lying just below the surface! The study presented in this book will look at the layers of Esther and reveal that the story, while historically true, is also God's parable about us, picturing the life of our inner man.

Before we get into the book, perhaps it would be helpful to review some frequently asked questions about bible study.

HOW IMPORTANT IS IT TO STUDY GOD'S WORD?

What does God's word, the scriptures, do for us?

1. We are sanctified (set apart for God's purposes, matured in our faith) through His Word.

"Sanctify them by Your truth, your WORD is truth," ~John 17:17.

2. God's Word makes us strong – it makes us overcomers. *"I have written unto you, young men, because you are strong, AND THE WORD OF GOD abides in you, and you have overcome the wicked one,"* ~I John 1:14.

3. According to Jesus, knowing and understanding the scriptures is imperative to being His disciple. Only God's Word is the truth that will set us free. *"IF you abide in MY WORD, you are my disciple indeed, and you shall know the truth and the truth shall make you free,"* ~John 8:31, 32.

4. Through the scriptures, we learn to know Jesus, and it is in Him that we have eternal life. *"You search THE SCRIPTURES, for in them you think you have eternal life; and these are they which testify of Me,"* ~John 5:39. And again we read, *"And this is the testimony; that God has given us eternal life, and this life is in His Son".* ~I John 5:11.

5. Hiding God's Word in our hearts, keeps us from sinning. *"Your WORD I have hidden in my heart, that I might not sin against You",* ~Psalm 119:11.

These are a few of the many scriptures that stress the importance, and personal benefit of studying God's Word. Read Psalm 119, sometime, with paper and pencil in hand and jot down all the benefits meditating on God's Word will give you.

WHAT HAS CHANGED TO AFFECT THE ATTITUDE OF CHRISTIANS REGARDING THE BIBLE?

Today we have multiple copies of the Bible in our homes and more versions and translations than we can keep up with. We have more access to books, Bible study helps, DVDs, online articles, and YouTube or video teaching than ever before – yet the Bible itself is read less than our forefathers would ever have believed possible. When it IS read, it is read often only as a devotional book, rather than studied as the exclusive authority on the truth that governs all things. God's word provides doctrinal truth, as well as practical truth, instructing us on how to live in every aspect of our physical and spiritual lives.

Today's accepted mind set, too often, takes the view that truth is relevant rather than absolute, subjective rather than objective, and personal opinions are valid and relevant in determining what is right and what is wrong. Feelings, and emotions, are more important than facts. The level of education, divides the wise from the unwise. The popularly accepted thought is that all religions have God's truth, all roads ultimately lead to God, and modern mysticism is fast gaining acceptance in our Christian churches and institutions. And so, in the mind of many Christians, consciously or otherwise, the Bible is an outdated book - often left on the shelf - and man's glossier, more palatable fare, is increasingly influencing the thoughts and belief systems of today's believers.

A quote by John Lawton, well known English author, is sadly true about our age, "The irony of the Information Age is that it has given new respectability to uninformed opinion." When we no longer look to God as the Source of all truth, then we no longer have any standard to measure truth by, other than popular opinion.

Medical science is raising the alarm that we are losing our health due to unhealthy eating habits, and the added chemicals to our over processed food. The alarm also needs to be raised on a spiritual level because we are allowing other voices to so fill our minds, that God's word is not given due attention, leaving us spiritually weak and vulnerable.

WHO CAN UNDERSTAND GOD'S WORD?

Often I hear the complaint, that the Bible is too difficult to understand, or is filled with stories that happened in a culture distantly removed from ours, or that much of the teaching just doesn't fit with our modern world view. But that is a lie of the enemy, because he knows that if he can keep someone from studying God's word - and believing it - he has that person in a vulnerable state where his lies and deception will find fertile ground.

The Bible is as relevant today, and as personally applicable, and as every-word-true, as it was the day God dictated it to the scribes recording His words. So who can understand this ancient book? Who still understands God's words and ways?

The Child - God is not a respecter of persons, and it was His delight to make His truth available to everyone, regardless of their degree of intelligence, or level of education, or social status, or any other worldly accolades that would elevate people in the eyes of others.

Hear the words of Jesus, *"I praise you, Father, Lord of heaven and earth, that you have hidden these things for the wise and prudent and revealed them to babes, even so Father, for so it seemed good in Your sight,"* ~Luke 10:21. We are told that Jesus rejoiced in this fact - that God's truth can be explained to, and understood by, a child! Jesus said, *"Let the little children come unto me!"* ~Luke 18:16.

The Seeker - God will reveal Himself and His truth to anyone who seeks Him. He promises that, if you lack the wisdom to understand, you need only ask for it to be given to you.

> *"But without faith it is impossible to please Him, for he who comes to God must believe that He is, and that He is a rewarder of those who diligently seek Him,"* ~Hebrews 11:6.

"If any of you lacks wisdom let him ask of God, who gives to all liberally and without reproach and it will be given to him!" ~James 1:5.

Those Who Have the Spirit of God - God has given every born-again believer His indwelling Holy Spirit, who guides, directs, and teaches. This is not to say that we do not have - or need - teachers who help us understand and learn, but the Spirit within us is our witness, whether or not a teaching we hear is from God or whether it is in error. We need to learn to recognize and heed this 'inner voice' to keep us diligent - testing and discerning the things we hear and believe. Nothing that is from God will ever contradict what we read in the Bible.

"But the anointing which you have received from Him abides in you and you do not need that anyone teach you, but as the same anointing teaches you concerning all things and is truth and is not a lie and just as it has taught you, you will abide in Him," ~I John 2:27.

The One Who Makes Knowing God His Life-focus - God wants our understanding of Him to be what we 'boast' about. If God wants us to 'boast or glory' about understanding Him, then He must surely have made it possible for us to do that, if we are diligent.

"Let not the wise man glory in his wisdom, let not the mighty man glory in his might, nor let the rich man glory in his riches, but let him who glories glory in this, that he understands and know me...That I am the Lord, exercising lovingkindness, judgement and righteousness in the earth. For in this I delight, says the Lord," ~Jeremiah 9:23, 24. (see also II Tim. 2:15)

WHAT TEACHING METHOD IS BEST SO EVERYONE LEARNS?

"One picture is worth ten thousand words." This phrase was coined for an advertising campaign for baking soda in the 1920's. Their philosophy was that if they put a picture of a happy, smiling, boy on the front of the box, people would be eager to run out and buy the product, which had the power to produce that smile! The implied message was – *If you want your boy to be happy, you need this product in your home.*

While man may have coined the actual phrase, the truth in the statement actually originated with God. It is the One who created man who best understands how man learns. Experts in the field of how people learn, have determined that learning styles can be divided into four main categories: Visual, Auditory, Kinesthetic and Tactile. Those who are visual learners, learn best through what they see, auditory learners learn best through what they hear, kinesthetic learners learn best through role playing or games and tactile learners benefit most by being involved hands on – acting, doing, experiencing.

But there is ONE method of teaching that allows everyone to learn regardless of their learning style. The teacher that teaches through stories reaches the mind of everyone listening. The intended lesson is presented in a way that allows every student to be able to understand, absorb, and remember.

Watch a congregation some Sunday during the sermon - you will see that some are reading their bulletin, some are dozing, the children are squirming, and others are staring off into space. Then, the pastor begins to tell an interesting story, and immediately you can sense the change in attentiveness of old and young alike. All eyes are riveted on the pastor. And it is most likely that it is the story that will be remembered and repeated later around the dinner table.

Jesus is recognized, by Christian and atheist alike, as the greatest teacher who ever walked this earth. Why? Because he understood how to 'capture His audience'. He taught through stories or pictures - parables or allegories.

This is what was said about Jesus' teaching, *"All these things Jesus spoke to the multitude in parables, and without a parable He did not speak to them, that it might be fulfilled which was spoken by the prophet, saying, I will open My mouth in parables ...,"* Matthew 13:34,35.

Jesus also declared that He spoke only what He heard

the Father say, *"As my Father taught me, I speak these things,"* John 8:28. And again, *"I speak what I have seen with my Father,"*~ John 8:38.

If Jesus' taught only what He heard the Father say, and if He never taught without parables, then does it not follow logically that 'parables' have always been God's preferred method of teaching truth to His children? If God truly is no respecter of persons, then He would have to purposely choose to teach in a way that ALL could learn. Even in His creation, God's character is displayed in 'picture' form. *"For since the creation of the world His invisible attributes are clearly seen, being understood by the things that are made..."* ~Romans 1:19. To observe God's visible creation is to observe His invisible character.

IS THE OLD TESTAMENT
RELEVANT FOR TODAY?

I remember reading Acts 20:7-12 as a child, and it always left me feeling intensely curious. This passage tells of Paul holding a captive audience with a sermon that lasted all night. What could Paul have possibly been talking about, that so fascinated his listeners that no one wanted to go home? I sensed, that Paul's sermon was not comparable to the sermons I was accustomed to hearing Sunday morning. Sermons I simply endured, wishing for and waiting for the benediction. But, here, the people were still listening hours into the sermon. Even the boy who obviously stayed up long past his bedtime didn't want to miss anything Paul said, but then, when he could stay awake no longer, he fell out of the window to his death. That would have ended most sermons, I'm sure. But no, not Paul's - someone simply brought the boy's dead body to Paul, who raised him back to life and carried on with his sermon for a few more hours, until morning dawned. If a miracle of raising someone from the dead, was not enough to detract from Paul's teaching, but was rather viewed only as a brief interruption, how I wished, I, too, could have been there to hear the spellbinding words of Paul.

What WAS Paul teaching about? Can we possible know? We have a clue in Acts 17:11 where Paul commends the Bereans because they were sincere seekers of the truth. They searched the scriptures daily to 'test' what Paul was saying. The verse reads, ***"These were more fair-minded than those in Thessalonica, in that they received the word with all readiness, and searched the Scriptures daily to find out whether these things were so."***

We make two common mistakes when we read this verse casually.

First, we judge the Bereans to be overly skeptical. If they could not take the apostle Paul at his word, who would they believe?

And the second thing we don't stop to think about, is that it was not the New Testament they were searching to test Paul's new doctrine. At that time there was no New Testament. All they had was the OLD TESTAMENT. So how DID they test the truth of Paul's teaching by the Old Testament scriptures?

There is only one possible answer. Paul's teaching conveyed the gospel message of the new covenant - his teaching would eventually be recorded to become several books of our own New Testament. If the Bereans were using the Old Testament scriptures to prove the truth of what Paul was saying, then Paul's gospel must have been hidden in the Old Testament. It has been poetically said, "The New is in the Old concealed, the Old is in the New revealed."

Jesus Himself, after His resurrection, when He was walking with two disciples along the way to Emmaus, 'opened' the scriptures to them, by showing them how it all spoke about Him! *"And beginning at Moses and all the Prophets He expounded to them in all the scriptures and things concerning Himself,"* ~Luke 24:37.

Could it be that God caused the stories of the Old Testament Israelites to be recorded in such a way, that they were 'parables or allegories' explaining in physical pictures the truths and doctrines that we study today in our New Testament? There are verses that give proof to that very fact. But, before we look at the proof scriptures, let us clarify some biblical terms that may, or may not, be familiar to you.

WHAT DO THESE BIBLICAL TERMS MEAN?

While the following terms are oft used interchangeably, there is a subtlety of difference in their meaning, which I hope I can make clear. Please note: Some of the terms are used in some Bible translations and not in others.

Parable - a narrative, a story using familiar circumstances and common things that are meant to have an abstract spiritual application. When we hear the word parable, we immediately think of the parables of Jesus, recorded in the gospels. Not all stories are parables, but all parables are stories.

Allegory – like a parable, in that physical things are given spiritual meanings, but an allegory is usually more complex in its symbolism. (For example – If you read the story of Sarah and Hagar in the book of Genesis, you do not 'see' any intended allegorical meaning. It is only when you are given the 'code words' of interpretation, in Gal. 4:24, that you realize there is a spiritual meaning that you would not see unless it was pointed out.)

Type and antitype - A type is something or someone that points to something or someone else. The antitype is the something or someone the type points to. For example in Romans 5:14, Adam is the type in that there are things about him that point to the coming Christ. Jesus is the one pointed to, and therefore he is the antitype. (See also I Peter 3:21) The cross of Jesus always stands between a type and its antitype. A type is always on the Old Testament side of the cross – before Jesus died - while an antitype is always on the New Testament side. (For another example, see I Peter 3:21.)

Copy/Shadow and good thing - the copy, or shadow, is something physical that foreshadows a spiritual reality (good thing) that is yet to come. The copy/shadow and good thing are the same as a type and antitype. In Col. 2:17, the copy/shadow is the type, the good thing is the antitype.

The antitype is always more important than the type. Using the copy/shadow analogy – the fact is that you cannot have a copy or a shadow if you do not have the original thing. You cannot make a copy of a document that has not been written, nor can you have a shadow of a tree that isn't there. So we know that Jesus and the New Covenant was always 'first' in God's mind and everything before Jesus was what was designed to 'point to' Him.

Example - a physical example of something spiritual yet to come. (see I Corinthians 10:11.)

Watch for these terms in the following proof scriptures.

WHAT PROOF SCRIPTURES DO WE HAVE THAT TELL US HOW WE ARE TO UNDERSTAND THE OLD TESTAMENT?

Romans 15:4 - *"For whatever things were written before were written for our learning, that we through the patience and comfort of the Scriptures might have hope."*

This verse is saying that the Old Testament stories of the Israelites contain spiritual truth that is specifically intended for us who are in the new covenant.

I Corinthians 10:11 - *"Now all these things happened to them as EXAMPLES and they were written for our admonition ON WHOM THE ENDS OF THE AGES HAVE COME."*

Again, the verse is clear. The experiences of the Israelites were recorded for OUR learning. And to leave no room for error in identifying the ones who were to follow 'the example', it states it is for those who live in the end times. We are closer to the end than anyone else has ever been, so it must be for us!

II Timothy 3:16 - *"All scripture is given by inspiration of God, and is profitable for doctrine, for reproof, for correction, for instruction in righteousness – that the man of God MAY BE COMPLETE, THOROUGHLY EQUIPPED FOR EVERY GOOD WORK!"*

When we read this verse, we automatically envision the New Testament, but when this verse was written there was no New Testament - the believers only had the Old Testament scrolls. Therefore, we must recognize that the Old Testament is profitable for doctrine, reproof, correction, instruction for us believers today!

Hebrews 8:5 - *"who [the priests] serve the COPY and SHADOW of the heavenly things, as Moses was divinely* *instructed when he was about to make the tabernacle, for He said, 'See that you make all things according to the pattern shown you on the mountain'."*

A very interesting concept here. The things of the Old Testament are a shadow. You cannot have a SHADOW unless there is a 'real thing' that casts the shadow. So if logic follows logic, the 'real thing' – the thing casting the shadow – must be first; therefore, in a very real way – in the mind of God - the New Covenant came first! God showed Moses the heavenly 'tabernacle', and told him to take care to build the copy/shadow of it exactly as it had been shown to him. It is a fascinating study to look at the symbolism of the tabernacle how it points to Jesus, and the New Covenant believer.

Galatians 4:24 - *"Which thing is an allegory, for these ARE the two covenants."* (verses 22-30)

Here we have a concrete example of how to interpret the Old Testament stories allegorically. It does not say, 'we could draw an interesting parallel here, or this reminds us of ...', but it states 'these ARE the two covenants'. This story, while it took place in real time, is recorded in such a way that it allegorically pictures the two covenants – the old and the new.

Considering the above passages, we can begin to understand why Paul's sermon was so fascinating to his listeners. Paul was telling the familiar Old Testament stories, and then revealing how the spiritual truths were hidden below the surface. The hidden truths were a mystery until Jesus came and the spiritual meanings were revealed

The Old Testament prophets knew that it was not for themselves that they were 'living out' the physical details of their lives, but that it was for a future generation, and they were very curious to know what it all meant. We are told in I Peter 1:10-,12, *"Of this salvation the prophets have inquired and searched diligently, who prophesied of the grace that would come to you, searching what or what manner of time the Spirit of Christ who was in them was indicating…… to them it was revealed that – not to themselves, but to us!, they were ministering the things which now have been reported to you through those who have preached the gospel to you by the Holy Spirit sent from heaven, things which angels desire to look into."*

CAN WE LOOK AT AN EXAMPLE OF HOW PAUL WOULD HAVE TAUGHT?

We read in John 3:**14**, *"And as Moses lifted up the serpent in the wilderness, even so must the Son of Man be lifted up."*

Reading this verse, it is easy to simply take it at face value - understanding it to say nothing more than making the point that Jesus was lifted up on a cross. But when we go to the picture story in Numbers 21:4-9 and look at it allegorically, we find the eyes of our understanding wonderfully enlightened.

The Israelites had sinned. Discouraged and angry, they grumbled against God and against Moses. God sent fiery serpents to punish them for their sin and the bite of the serpent was fatal. Then, when they cried out to God for deliverance, God commanded Moses to erect a bronze serpent, and everyone who simply 'looked' at the bronze serpent lived.

It is interesting to note that the Hebrew word used in verses six and eight in our Numbers passage, and is translated into our English 'bit' or 'bitten', is a word that means 'to strike with a sting'. Then when we go to I Corinthians 15:56, we see that Paul uses that word 'sting' in reference to sin, *"the sting of death is sin."* Using those code-words, the mystery of the analogy then unfolds. We are familiar with scripture references to Satan being called a serpent; therefore, we can see that the serpents that bit the people represent the sin that bites us and causes our death. When the serpent bit the people, they died. When Adam and Eve sinned and brought death upon the whole human race, we all, in turn, are bitten by sin and are condemned to die. Only when Jesus was lifted up on the cross did salvation come - people could look to Him and live!

I used to wonder why Moses was commanded to lift up a bronze serpent - after all, it was the serpent that was responsible for the death of the people. Why was it now commanded by God to be the instrument of giving life?

Then, I understood. It was sin that caused us to die,

and until our sin was lifted up on the cross of Jesus - placed upon Him - we could not have deliverance.

Though the bronze serpent had the power to give everyone life, simply lifting it up in the wilderness was not enough. Every person that was bitten had to look up at the bronze serpent believing that, as Moses had promised, it would give them life.

To live spiritually, each one of us must look up at the cross of Christ and see our own sin hanging there. And we must believe that only Jesus, through His supreme sacrifice, can save us. That is the conclusion we see in John 3:15, which follows the verse we began with, **"*And as Moses lifted up the serpent in the wilderness, even so must the Son of Man be lifted up,* that *whoever believes in Him should not perish but have eternal life'*.**

So we can see how Paul using the code words from John 3:14, unlocks the mystery of Numbers 21:4-9.

ARE THERE RULES FOR INTERPRETING SCRIPTURE ALLEGORICALLY?

1. Never interpret according to your own idea, imagination or belief system, or any code source outside of the bible. II Peter 1:20 **"*Knowing this first! That no prophecy of scripture is of any private interpretation."*** The New Testament is our 'code book' to help us find the hidden treasure in the Old Testament. Find the code breaker scripture, then decipher the lesson.

2. Not every detail in the earthly parable or story or event has to necessarily correspond to a spiritual meaning - some details are there only to make the story hang together.

3. No correct interpretation will ever contradict any clear teaching of scripture.

4. The correct interpretation will convey a spiritual truth that is taught elsewhere in scripture. God rarely says something only once. (Psalm 62:11, II Cor. 13:1)

COULD THE BOOK OF ESTHER BE GOD'S PARABLE TO NEW COVENANT BELIEVERS?

Some years ago, I was thinking about how Jesus said that He never spoke anything except what He heard His Father speak. That Jesus never taught without a parable was a fulfillment of the prophecy in Psalm 78:2, therefore, it was a very important aspect of His earthly ministry. The thought took hold of me that God, then, would also have had to teach by parable, otherwise Jesus could not have heard it from Him. Where in the Old Testament could this be seen? Where was there a parable of God? I wondered, could it be the book of Esther? I noted how the book of Esther had the same parable markers as are consistent in Jesus' parables.

- **Characters are not named** - Jesus often introduced a parable by saying, "there was a certain man….."

as He does in Luke 20:9. Then He began to tell the people this parable, "A certain man planted a vineyard ...." In a parable, the main characters are not names because the listener is meant to insert his own name since the message is about him.

- **God is never mentioned in a parable** - if you look at Jesus' parables, you will note that God is not mentioned in any of them, nor is there reference to anything spiritual.
- **The interpretation is about the Kingdom of God and our spiritual life** - when Jesus explained the meaning of His parable, He pointed out how the pieces of His parable represented some spiritual truth pertaining to the kingdom of God

Unless God recorded the book of Esther, as a parable with hidden spiritual meaning, why would this book be included in the Bible? It does not mention God, nor does it mention heaven, or hell, nor does it have any prophetic words about the coming Messiah.

> **AN INTERESTING NOTE** - I choose the title for my book **"The Megillah of Esther"** for a reason. The Feast of Purim, is one of the Jew's yearly feasts, and as part of the celebration, tradition demands the reading of the story of Esther. In ancient times, the scriptures were recorded, not in books, but on scrolls. So if the story of Esther was to be read, the scroll

containing the story would be asked for. But because each scroll, containing the words of God was seen as the revelation of the word of God - the Hebrew word for scroll was not used - rather they used the word for 'revelation' which was Megillah. Therefore, when the scroll of Esther was needed what was asked for was "The Megillah of Esther". Names in the Bible are important, often holding hidden clues pertaining to the life of the named character, his character traits, key events, or his place in history. The Hebrew word for Esther means 'hidden'. Therefore, when a Jew sees, or hears, the words, "The Megillah of Esther", he thinks *... "revelation of that which is hidden".* From ancient times, the Jews have believed that Esther is an allegory, or parable, with hidden meaning. Jews have argued and debated and tried to unravel the hidden truths, but since they have rejected the code-breaker, they have not been able to solve the mystery. We, however, DO have the code-breaker – we who believe in Jesus and have the New Testament scriptures and we are able to discover how wonderfully its allegorical meaning can be revealed.

IS THE BOOK OF ESTHER
HISTORICALLY TRUE?

While I believe that Esther is a historically accurate account of real events, not everyone agrees. There are several views that are put forward regarding the book of Esther. They are as follows:

1. That the book of Esther is the recording of real life events in history.

2. That it is a fable based on mythology with the characters' names made to closely resemble Greek gods and goddesses. For example, it is argued that since Mordecai is not a Jewish name, it must be a derivative of the Greek god Marduk.

3. That the author used his extensive knowledge of Persian law and custom to weave a fascinating story.

4. That if this account is about Xerxes I, then historical facts do not match. For example, Xerxes' queen was Amestris, not Vashti, and the account of the palace intrigue and Esther becoming queen are not found recorded by any historians.

Before I briefly address these views, let me emphasis that even though men recorded the scriptures and men translated them from the original languages, it is a small thing for God to watch over His word to make sure His truth is preserved and protected from error. Thus, for me, the very fact that the book of Esther is included in the pages of my Bible is enough to convince me that God meant for it to be there - therefore, I do not have to wonder if it is true. I know it is, and it is worthy of my study.

Some of the above listed objections to the historical accuracy of Esther are easily addressed. To say that it is a fable is simply someone's opinion with no supporting fact. To say it is someone's story woven around their intimate knowledge of Persian law is farfetched, again, with no supporting evidence. To those who deny that Mordecai is a Jewish name, let them turn to Nehemiah 7:7 and see that the name is included in the list of returning Jews to Jerusalem.

The one objection that does have some reasonable merit and therefore invites examination, is the question of who the King of Persia was at that time, since the names used in the biblical account do not match any secular historical records.

Recognized and respected scholars seem to agree that this Ahasuerus, the king in Esther's story, is the historical Xerxes I. There are more parallels between what we know about Xerxes I and what we are told about the King in Esther than for any other Persian ruler. We are not given any time frame in the book of Esther, but it is reasonable to fit it into the time of Xerxes I's reign from 486-465 BC. We know Xerxes I disposed his queen in 482 BC. We know of a huge event he put on to show off this power and affluence. We know that after a stunning defeat against the Greek army, Xerxes I went home defeated and determined to avoid war, choosing instead to indulge himself in a palace life-style of wine, women and feasting.

What we know of Xerxes I, seems to fit the details we are given about the King of Esther.

But ... the King of Esther is called Ahasuerus, not Xerxes. This is really not the problem that it would appear to be. Ahasuerus means prince, head, chief - a title like Emperor, or Caesar. As we shall see, there is a reason the King's given name is not referred to in our biblical account. (a) (b) (c)

CAN WE CONCLUDE THAT ESTHER PASSES THE PARABLE TEST?

Earlier I listed the marks of a parable - a story where the main character is not named, God is not named nor mentioned, nor is anything of a spiritual nature referred to. We find those marks fitting the story of Esther and just as Jesus opened His parable with, "There was a certain man ..." so also the book of Esther begins its story with, "Now it came to pass in the days (of a certain man) ...." Unlike most parables, the book of Esther is historically true, but it is a fascinating account with the facts recorded in such a way that it holds the mystery of a parable just waiting to be solved.

CHAPTER ONE

Seeking the Good Life

Esther 1:1-8

These events happened in the time of Ahasuerus, who ruled over a hundred and twenty-seven provinces from India to Ethiopia 2from his royal throne in the fortified palace of Susa. 3In the third year of his reign, the king gave a feast for all his officers and courtiers. The commanders of the military forces of Persia and Media, the nobles and provincial rulers were present 4while for one hundred and eighty days he showed them the glorious riches of his kingdom and the costliness of his magnificent regalia. 5When these days were ended, the king held a banquet for all the people who were present in the royal palace at Susa, high and low alike. It was a seven days' feast in the enclosed garden of the royal palace. 6There were white and violet cotton curtains fastened to silver rings and pillars of marble with cords of fine purple wool and linen. The couches were of gold and silver placed upon a mosaic pavement of alabaster, white marble, mother-of-pearl, and dark stone. 7Drink was brought in vessels of gold --- which were all different --- and the king's wine was provided with royal liberality. 8The drinking was unrestricted, for the king had directed all the officers of his household to let each man do as he pleased.

"Now it came to pass in the days of Ahasuerus ...." So the parable begins.

As we open our study of Esther as a parable, the first question that must be answered is who, or what, Ahasuerus represents in this parable. He is the key to unlocking the mystery hidden in our story. Ahasuerus is the main character on stage, not Esther, though the book is named for her.

Puzzle Pieces

My parents are avid puzzlers. They have put more puzzles together than I could count. When they begin a puzzle, they will often place within the finished border some unique piece that seems to have an obvious place in the puzzle. That position will be proven to be correct if the other pieces of the puzzle fit into place around it. In a puzzle, every piece must find its place for the puzzle to be successfully completed to mirror the picture the puzzle was made from. A puzzle is really an exercise in working backwards, to put together again the 'whole' from which each piece is a part. A parable is like that as well. The parable begins with the truth it will illustrate ... then the pieces of that truth are woven into the parable or story. Listening to the parable, the hearer must work backwards, taking the pieces and clues of the puzzle to put back together again the original message the parable creator was wanting to convey through his story.

Placing Ahasuerus as an obvious, eye catching piece in our parable puzzle is like that first piece that has not yet had its correct position proven. I will tell you who Ahasuerus is, but you may rightly question how I know - after all, I don't even have the picture on the puzzle box! I know where the Ahasuerus-piece fits, because I have already put the puzzle together, and I have found that all the other pieces fit around the identity I assign to Ahasuerus. I was able to satisfactorily complete the puzzle with no ill-fitting pieces and no pieces left over nor any pieces missing.

So if you will, follow along with me and watch as I start with Ahasuerus and then, one by one, add the other puzzle pieces of the parable. I believe you will see by the way they all fall into place that it cannot be by mere conjecture or co-incidence.

Who is Ahasuerus?

Ahasuerus, in our parable, represents the center of our being - our will - the throne where we sit and rule our life, where choices, and decisions are made based on the information we receive and evaluate.

The parable of Esther is the story of you and me - a

3

story 'picture-book', revealing who we are. We are body, soul, and spirit in our earthly life. On the stage of this parable, we will see played out for us an objective view of how we, as a tri-une being, relate to the physical and spiritual world in which we have our inner life. The story of Esther holds up to us a mirror, not the kind of mirror that reflects back to us the outward physical features that allow us to recognize and identify people by name, but a divine mirror that allows us to see ourselves from the inside out. A mirror that reveals the invisible reality of who we are - that 'inner man' part of us that is eternal. It is interesting to note that the Merriam-Webster dictionary gives as the original Latin root of the word 'parable', the meaning "to place alongside for the purpose of comparing."

The Bible uses the image of a mirror and connects it a promise in II Corinthians 3:18. This verse tells us that if we will look into the mirror that God has given us - His Word - we will be changed to look like the glorious image of the Lord. ***"But we all, with unveiled face, beholding as in a mirror, the glory of the Lord, are being transformed into the same image from glory to glory, just as by the Spirit of the Lord."***

Oh ... this is so much better a promise than the promises of a new diet or even plastic surgery to improve our outer image, but it might be just as painful in the process. As we gaze into the 'mirror' that the parable of Esther holds up to us, we may not always like what we see, especially when we realize that the cure involves the pain of a surgeon's knife in our soul. But rather than shrink back, let us focus on the glory of who we will be and willingly submit to the changes we must make.

We have noted, in the introduction, that Ahasuerus is not a given name, but rather a title, like Pharaoh, or ruler, or prince - again, this fits with the marks of a parable. Ahasuerus is, "a certain man, who rules as a king", and if we accept that Esther is a parable, we must then follow the rules of a parable and study the parable on a personal level, identifying with it as though our own name is written there.

The Kingdom

Another detail about Ahasuerus, that supports the story of Esther being understood as a parable of our inner self, is that, throughout the story, Ahasuerus never leaves his fortified palace, or citadel, in Susa or Shushan, just as we never leave our physical bodies. Everything we perceive, everything we do in our life, we do from within the confines of our physical bodies, and we cannot step outside of it. And just as Ahasuerus sits on the throne that is in his palace, so 'our will' sits on the throne from where our whole being is ruled. The story of Esther makes no reference to anything outside of Ahasuerus' kingdom - nothing beyond what Ahasuerus directly rules over. Since we know that we cannot rule over anything outside of our own body, we have defined that our parable is contained within the 'kingdom' of our physical body and nothing in the parable represents anything outside of the body. Since our awareness of who we are and where we think and reason is in our minds or head, we could perhaps link the palace with our mind. However, for the purpose of the parable, the terms, palace, citadel, king's house, Susa or Shushan are all closely related, and interchangeable, and our total being - body, soul, and spirit - is understood to be included in the term 'kingdom'.

In verse one, we are told that Ahasuerus reigned, or ruled, over one hundred and twenty-seven provinces. In recent years the study of our brain and how it rules over our body has revolutionized medical science's understanding of the subject. I have been fascinated by Dr. Caroline Leaf's study of the brain, along with others who have supported and built on her studies. It has been proven that so much of what goes on in our body, and the working of our body functions as well as our emotional or mental well-being, originates with our thoughts - what we choose, or 'will', to think about. In Dr. Leaf's book, *Who Switched Off My Brain*, she says, "What you think and feel prompts your hypothalamus to begin a series of chemical secretions that change the way you function," (pg. 23). If this is true, then Ahasuerus ruling over 127 provinces, is saying that from our will, we rule over our kingdom that comprises our body, soul, and spirit. Do we rule over our body in 127 different functions, or ways? I don't know, but it would be most interesting if medical science proved that the numbers did match up! However, what we do know is that we have a direct and willful rule over our kingdom which is comprised of the aspects of our physical and spiritual life.

Is it important to recognize this authoritative power

of our will? Yes, I believe that it is. It is the gift that God gave mankind, the freedom of choice - the power, the authority, and right to make our own decisions, to rule our life as we see fit. Having a free will, we sit on the throne of our SELF.

Ahasuerus, and his palace, are described in glowing terms. We read phrases like, "riches of his glorious kingdom" and "splendor of his excellent majesty". Verse six describes the breathtaking décor of the palace. (a)

Don't these descriptive words almost leave you breathless - *"a mosaic pavement of alabaster, white marble, mother-of-pearl, and dark stone"*? What could the meaning of these parable details be but the description of our created being? Does Psalm 139:14 not describe us in similar terms?

> *"I will praise you, for I am fearfully and wonderfully made, marvelous are your works and that my soul knows very well. My frame was not hidden from you, when I was made in secret and skillfully wrought ...."*

And then we read these unbelievable words in Psalm 45:11, *"So the King will greatly desire your beauty, because He is your Lord, worship Him."* Next time you look in the mirror, remember that it does not have the capability to reflect the true beauty that God sees in you ... beauty that He created in you because you are made in His image ... beauty He desires to reveal in and through you.

Just as each of the guests at Ahasuerus' banquet had a unique vessel to drink from so God has not only created each of us a uniquely designed vessel, or person, but has also given us – within our physical bodies - a unique set of personality traits and abilities that He desires to fill with the light and glory and purpose of God. ***"But we have this treasure in earthen vessels, that the excellency of the power may be of God and not of us,"*** ~II Corinthians 4:7. (b)

So in reading the details of the splendor of Ahasueres' palace, we are reminded, in no uncertain terms, that when God created Adam and Eve, He pronounced them 'good'. I believe even Solomon's palace would pale in any attempted comparison. We have only to study the physical body to be amazed at the wondrous ways in which it works. In Dr. Paul Brand's book, *In the Likeness of God*, he describes, from a surgeon's intimate point of view, the intricacies of the human body, and it is enough to awe us into silence.

It is an interesting detail to note that the meaning of Shushan, or Susa – the name of the palace, or citadel, where Ahasuerus lived - is "whiteness". Man was created perfect, since God could create nothing less. Adam was "white" in his beauty and sinlessness - no wicked thought had ever crossed his mind. Then Adam fell, bringing sin and death into this world. Sin soiled and tarnished man as God's perfect creation, but it is in 'white' that God, once again, wishes to clothe us. Look at Revelation 3:18, and

4:4, that speak of the 'white garments' of the saints. We, as believers, are not only clothed in white robes but are also white in our sinlessness, having been washed clean in the blood of the Lamb. Incredibly, God desires for us to look like Jesus. In Mark 9:3, when Jesus was revealed to the disciples in His transfigured state, we read, ***"His clothes became shining, exceedingly white, like snow, such as no launderer on earth can whiten them."*** Don't you long to wear a garment like that?

The Worth of Man in God's Eyes

The parable opens with God's view of man, in all his beauty and perfection - though even the best of us struggle to believe that this is personally true, and rarely do we dare to believe in our full potential. And though we often compare ourselves unfavorably with others, we do, however, instinctively know that we have worth and value - more than others recognize us for. The Bible says, in Ephesians 5:29, ***"For no one ever hated his own flesh, but nourishes and cherishes it."*** We may be tempted to point out that we are suffering from poor self-esteem, or even that we despise ourselves, but is it not because we feel 'less than' that these negative emotions are stirred and we are so disconcerted? The very fact that we are aware of some inner lack, shows that we know we are worthy of more.

However, Ahasuerus shows no issues with his self-esteem. The first thing we see him doing is throwing a party, ***"in abundance according to the generosity of the***

king. This is a party that goes on, not for a few hours, but, incredibly, for one hundred and eighty days. Then, when these days come to an end, Ahasuerus isn't finished partying, so he simply calls for another seven day revelry. We understand the phrase 'indulging the flesh', and we see that Ahasuerus' generosity to himself has no limits. He is living the good life – or is he?

How many feasts have we thrown for our own pleasure? How often do we think of what will entertain us or give us pleasure for a few minutes, an evening, or a week or two on vacation? Do we not do everything we can to indulge ourselves - to provide first and foremost for the comfort that caters to the desires and self-satisfaction of our flesh? Is it not ME FIRST, and then, in our generosity, give of any leftovers to others? It is this nature in us that Jesus pointed to when He gave us the commandment to love others and gave us very specific directions for the 'HOW-TO'. The way we love ourselves - that is our standard, our inbred experience on how we are to love others. We can all recite Jesus' golden rule, ***"And just as you want men to do to you, you also do to them likewise,"*** ~Luke 6:31. We don't have to learn how to love. We already know how, we just need to shift our love focus onto others, instead of hoarding it in order to consume it on loving ourselves.

What is the Good Life?

Look at the interesting law Ahasuerus enforced in his kingdom - that no one was to be denied. Everyone was to be allowed to do exactly as he pleased! That is so obvious, it makes us blush with shame. Really? If we are willing to admit it or not, is that not a law we have on the first page of our own law-book? If we can get away with it, we declare that no part of us has to do anything contrary to what we want to do. I think of I John 1:16, ***"For all that is in the world – the lust of the flesh, the lust of the eyes, and the pride of life …."*** That is really the 'feast' we throw for ourselves. In everything, our first carnal thought is self-ward as we look to fulfill our own pleasure. We seek the good life – and define it as a life of ease and prosperity.

CHAPTER TWO

The Spirit of Man

Esther 1:9 – 12

Queen Vashti also gave a feast for the women in the royal palace (belonging to) King Ahasuerus. 10On the seventh day, when the king was merry with wine, he commanded Mehuman, Biztha, Harbona, Bigtha, Abagtha, Zathar and Carkas, his seven eunuch attendants 11to bring Queen Vashti before him with the royal diadem on her head, to show her beauty to the people and the officials, for she was very beautiful. 12But Queen Vashti refused to come as the king commanded through the eunuchs. Then the king became very angry and his fury burned within him.

A Queen named Vashti

We are introduced to the second character - Vashti. Who is she? She is Ahasuerues' queen but in secular accounts of Persian history, there is no reference to a Queen named

Vashti, which is one of the reasons scholars give as proof that Esther is not a historical book. Since we have already established that Ahasuerus is not a given name but rather a title, it would be reasonable to conclude that his queen would also be referred to by a title rather than a given name. (a)

Vashti means 'beautiful, lovely' or 'best, excellent'. She is the queen, the wedded wife of the king. A Persian King, having a harem of women who all lived together in separate women's quarters, did not allow any of his wives or concubines to eat at his table except his mother and his queen. (b) Considering this fact, we can see that Vashti would be a title that immediately identified her as having the status of this privileged wife, a title that would separate her from the other women of the King's harem.

So, if Ahasuerus is our will, who does Vashti represent? As queen, she is the 'life' of the king, because he can have no heirs to his kingdom without her. Therefore, Vashti represents our spirit, the part of us that gives us life - both here in this earthly life and beyond physical death. It is what sets us apart from the animals and gives us the ability to communicate with the Spirit of God, in whose image we were created. Our spirit, God-given breath and life, is 'beautiful'.

We are told that Vashti lives in the palace belonging to Ahasuerus. This detail provides us with a clue about the relationship between the queen and Ahasuerus. She lives in the palace, and since we have already established that the palace is in the kingdom of our physical body, we see that our spirit also abides in the body. It might seem

13

odd to us that we are told the queen lives in the palace that belongs to the king; in our minds we would expect it to belong to both of them. But because of this careful wording, we must pay attention to it, recognizing that it indicates that Ahasuerus alone rules in HIS palace. Therefore, we understand that our spirit is subject to, or under the rule of, our will. Can we prove this is true? We can, with I Corinthians 14:32, which says, ***"And the spirits of the prophets are subject to the prophets."***

This verse states that even when the Spirit of God is speaking to His prophet, the man's spirit (through which he hears God's message) is subject to the will of the man. So, we must conclude that our will rules over our spirit. It has often been said that God is a gentleman and never forces us to do or accept anything contrary to our will. We see that pictured here in our parable - Vashti is in the palace **belonging to** Ahasuerus, who alone rules over his kingdom and nothing happens without his knowledge and willful consent.

But wait, you say … if Ahasuerus, or our will, rules over our spirit, then why did Vashti not obey the king's order? The answer is that Ahasuerus is asking something of Vashti that she cannot do without endangering her life. In the same way, we cannot violate our spirit. Let me present the reasoning I worked through that led me to this conclusion.

We read that Vashti also makes a feast for the women in the palace. Note the word ALSO. What does that signify? Vashti is watching what Ahasuerus is doing, and she follows his example, not the other way around. Our spirit is affected by, and reflects, what we 'will' to do in our decisions, as well as what we 'will' in choosing our moral and ethical standard.

In the Old Testament, we read of a man having a jealous spirit. Which came first? His judgment of his wife's behavior or a jealous spirit? Obviously, the husband saw something regarding his wife's behavior that made him question her fidelity. His 'will' in how he judged her, whether or not he had just cause, permeated his thoughts and actions until it was reflected in his spirit. We are told he had a jealous 'spirit', because his jealousy became all-consuming. (Numbers 3:11-31)

Returning to our parable and considering what we just concluded - that Vashti follows what she sees Ahasuerus do - then how we see the parable events unfold, seems to contradict that conclusion. If Vashti reflects what she sees Ahasuerus do, then why do we see her disobeying and doing contrary to what Ahasuerus demanded of her? And truly, the command - to our modern way of thinking - seems to be a rather sweet, complimentary request that Ahasuerus makes of his queen. He wants to show her off, brag about her. Most wives would not be offended at their husbands taking pride in them. But there is something more involved here in our Persian palace scene, something that we would miss if we do not understand Persian law and custom. The king was not simply asking his queen to come greet his guests and join them for a drink.

Laws/Customs of Persia

Let's look at some of the Persian laws or customs that will insure a correct understanding of the interaction between Ahasuerus and Vashti.

1. Modesty was very important to Persian women. A wife or queen would not even eat at her husband's table if men she did not know would be present.

2. Higher cast Persian women, and especially royalty, were veiled and were not ever seen in public. They were very carefully guarded in seclusion. Lower caste women and prostitutes were not veiled. (c)

3. What a man said or did or even decreed when he was drunk, was not enforced by Persian law. In fact, the next morning, when the man was again sober, he could retract or even go contrary to what he had done or promised to do in his drunken state. (d)

Now let us take a moment to look at how the above customs figure into our story. For a Persian woman to be unveiled in public or before men other than her husband was prohibited, not unlike the Islamic law that demands women to wear a burqa in public. (*An interesting side note is that the word burqa is an Arabized word from the Persian word purda. The Persian word, purda, and the Arabized word, burqa, both mean curtain and veil.*) A Persian woman who displayed herself in front of other men, was under penalty of death. Also we know Ahasuerus is drunk when he commands Vashti to come parade her beauty, immodestly, before Ahasuerus's male guests. Vashti knows that if she obeys, when Ahasuerus regains his sober mind, he will have her punished. So she refuses.

A Story from Secular History

There is an historical account of a story that supports my above opinion that Vashti had good reason to refuse her husband's command to 'show her beauty' to his guests.

> A Lydian king, (the Lydian and Persian kings shared common laws and customs), had a very beautiful wife whom he deeply loved. He had a servant by the name of Gyges. The king must have valued this man more than just as his servant because he desired Gyges to see how very beautiful his wife was. The Lydian custom was the same as in Persian law – that a woman who was judged to be immodest before men, faced the punishment of death. Because of this law, women were very careful to protect their modesty, and the king knew that his queen would not obey a command that would endanger her life. So the king came up with a devious plan that he thought would allow him to show off his queen's beauty to Gyges without compromising, or humiliating, his queen. The Lydian king hid Gyges in the master bedroom behind a curtain from where he could watch the queen undress. Then, he could quietly slip unnoticed

from the room, and the queen need never know she had been seen. The story records that, to his credit, Gyges tried desperately to refuse the king's offer, recoiling from the thought of dishonoring his queen. However, Candaules insisted, and finally Gyges was forced to give in. Things did not go according to plan - when he tried to slip unnoticed from the bedroom, the queen caught a glimpse of him and realized immediately what had happened. There was only one way to restore her honor and the angry queen forced Gyges to carry it out. Because it was Candaules who had betrayed her, he had to die. The queen forced Gyges to kill the king, then she married Gyges, who was shortly thereafter also murdered by palace insiders. (Source - Herodotus' Histories, book 1.7-12)

Queen Vashti – Guilty or Innocent?

Because of the way the story of Esther is told, most people hold the opinion that Vashti was disobedient and rebellious, but that is obviously not true. She was the one who was honorable in refusing to do what was immoral, unveiling herself. And considering that she knew Ahasuerus would have the law on his side to condemn her in the morning, she would have been motivated to refuse to do something that was punishable by death.

So what does this teach us about our spirit? Just as the queen, in refusing to appear before Ahasuerus, remains 'hidden', our spirit is also hidden. We cannot display or flaunt it. If we give power over our spirit to someone other than God, it will ultimately cause our death. Our spirit is a sensitive and vulnerable part of our being that we are meant to guard and we cannot force our spirit to be anything contrary to the purpose for which God intended it. We can, however, turn away from our spirit and silence its influence in our life.

Therefore, while our spirit reflects who we are in our will, it cannot be ordered by our will. There is a verse that would seem, at first reading, to contradict this.

"Whoever has no rule over his own spirit, is like a city broken down, without walls," ~Proverbs 25:28.

Does this not seem to imply that we do, and should, rule over our spirit and that our spirit must obey our will?

Most of us have vehicles that we use to take us where we need, or choose, to go. We learn how to drive, how to 'rule' over our car and use it to serve our needs. But if you put a child behind the wheel with the car running, it doesn't take much imagination to project the end result – **"a city broken down, without walls"**. We rule over our vehicle as long as we rule according to the laws of intended use and purpose. If we violate those laws, as in trying to force it to function as a boat, destruction will result because the vehicle cannot be made to do contrary to the mechanism built into it. So also our spirit cannot do what God did not create it to do.

Searing our Conscience

There is a tension between our spirit and our will, as we see pictured in the exchange between Vashti and Ahasuerus. Looking at a couple of verses will help us to understand what Ahasuerus' anger with Vashti revels about us.

Our spirits are the conduit through which we are able to communicate in the spiritual realms and directly with God. We read in Romans 8:16, ***"The Spirit Himself bears witness with our spirit that we are children of God."*** Here we see how we receive a message from God. In this verse, the message is the confirmation that we are a child of God. It comes from God through His Spirit to our spirit and then is communicated to our conscious mind.

In Romans 2:15, we read, ***"....their conscience also bearing witness and between themselves their thoughts accusing or else excusing them."***

And in Romans 9:1, Paul states, ***"I tell the truth in Christ, I am not lying, my conscience also bearing me witness in the Holy Spirit."***

The above quoted verses indicate that what we call our conscience is either a part of our spirit or part of our mind that is sensitive to what our spirit senses from God. God is able, through our conscience, to trouble us, convict us, or make us feel guilty, if we are ignoring or walking contrary to God's best for us, (Proverbs 20:27). Often we wish to switch our conscience off so it does not bother us when we want to walk according to our own ways and desires. Paul speaks to this in I Timothy 4:2, ***"...having their conscience seared with a hot iron."***

Just as we turn off or mute the TV when the commercials are too loud and annoying, so we can, in anger, turn off our 'reception' to our spirit or conscience - effectively rejecting their God-given purpose in our life.

An Offended King

Ahasuerus does not want to have his queen make him uncomfortable or deny him his drunken pleasure, so he is angry with her. Actually, we are told that his anger burns within him – it is all consuming. Not only has he been denied, he has also been greatly humiliated.

Do we not react negatively when we are denied? When our conscience bothers us, do we correct our path, or do we respond in anger? Do we seek to silence it when it plagues, or torments us, with guilt emotions? Do we not use every excuse in the book to justify what we desire to have, or do, and thereby find some kind of validation for our right to have, or do, as we wish?

This is what we see in Ahasuerus' actions, from the moment he conceives the desire to call Vashti into his presence. He does not pick up his cell phone and give Vashti a quick text message to come to the banquet hall. No, he sends out seven of his servants to go get her - not one, but seven! Does he, even in his drunken state, know that she will resist what he is asking of her? I think there is a significance in the number seven, since seven in the bible is symbolic of God's Divine completion and perfection. Could this little detail in the number of servants Ahasuerus sends out to do his bidding, indicate Ahasuerus is asserting his power of authority by sending out a convincing bevy of officials? Is it not something we, too, can be guilty of when we try to justify what we want to do and use some truth, or scripture, that taken out of context or given a little twist looks convincing, and, thereby, we think to soothe our conscience and validate our desire?

Ahasuerus, sends his seven eunuchs to compel Vashti to appear before him and his guests. A eunuch, by definition, is impotent - unable to give life. The analogy here is clear; these eunochs who serve the king, are unable to speak words of life, or wisdom, to Ahasuerus.

In the Bible names are important in that, more often than not, the meaning of the name speaks to some detail, or purpose, or character trait, of the person to whom the name is given. Adam was named Adam because he was formed from the earth, Eve was so named because she was the mother of all living. Abraham was so named because he was to be the father of many. We could do a side study looking at all the Bible names and see how their meanings add to our understanding, but we won't take the time here except as they relate to our parable.

It's All in the Name

We are given the names of the eunuchs that Ahasuerus called upon. They are: Mehuman, Biztha, Harbona, Bigtha, Abagtha, Zethar and Carcas. These are ancient

Persian names, and while it is difficult to know how perfectly the original meanings of these names have been preserved, I think the meanings I have found add a great deal of interest to our parable interpretation. (e)

Following is a list of Ahasuerus' eunuchs and the meaning of their names.

Mehuman - means 'making an uproar'. When we are prevented from getting our own way, is that not our most primal reaction, one we readily see from the time we are born? Make an uproar, complain loud enough, create enough chaos and fuss, and maybe someone will come and give us what we want.

Biztha - means 'despise, distain, show contempt'. Another tactic we use to justify what we want, we despise or show contempt for what is right or for anything that stands in our way.

Harbona - means 'his destruction, his sword'. We will do what we have to do to get what we want, even if we have to fight for it.

Bigtha - means 'in the press, giving meat' or 'fortune'. This is showing how our first consideration in demanding what we want is the consideration of what benefit it will offer us. Will it give us 'meat'? Will it give us 'fortune'?

Abagtha - means 'father of the wine press'. We turn away from reason or truth, and numb our minds with substance – wine, drugs, medication – so that we do not feel guilt or condemnation to hinder us in getting what we want.

Zethar - means 'he that examines or beholds'. Adam and Eve examined and beheld the temptation before them and found that it was good. If we examine and behold the thing that is wrong and see what it promises, we will be taken captive by it. So many sins begin with what we allow ourselves to 'behold'... be it the sins of covetousness or immorality. What is beautiful to the eyes and desirable cannot be sin, can it?

Carcas - means 'the covering of a lamb'. How aptly does this describe deception … a lie, an enemy seeking prey, an evil covered over with the wool of a lamb … we justify our sin so that it looks respectable. Jerry Bridges' book, *"Respectable Sins",* addresses this very 'Carcas' still lurking in our midst.

Considering the identity of the eunuchs just described, we understand that just like Ahasuerus sought 'lifeless' justifying excuses on why he should be allowed to do what he wanted to do, so we too call upon the same excuses to serve us in making us comfortable in our own sins of choice.

We see Ahasuerus is furious because he has been denied the fulfillment of his desire. We all relate to feeling anger when we are denied. We understand that the enemy's desire is to destroy God's work in His people, and we are told in Revelation 12:12 of his great wrath when Satan sees his schemes fail over and over. Yet, how easily we slip into following his example and act just like him. Jesus' words to the unredeemed are recorded in John 8:44, ***"You are of your father the devil, and the desires of your father you want to do …."***

CHAPTER THREE

Unwise Advisors

Esther 1:13, 14

The king turned to the wise men who knew the precedents, for it was his custom to confer with those wise in law. 14Those next to him were Carshena, Shethar, Admatha, Tarshish, Meres, Marsena and Memucan, seven officials of Persia and Media who had access to the king and were highest in the kingdom.

Call in the Support

When we are upset or angry or feel mistreated or denied, is our first reaction not to seek for support? We want to be right, we want to be confirmed, we want to be validated, listened to and told what we want to hear.

This is just what we see Ahasuerus doing. He turns to his wise men - those who are closest to him - the ones he can count on to come alongside him, speaking comforting words and making sure that the king is not seen in any negative light that might cast upon him some shadow of fault. We live in a society where we have a pervasive victim mentality and entitlement attitude; everything is someone else's fault.

Ahasuerus, in his day, already had this attitude. Maybe the problem is not so much the times we live in, but that this mindset is foundational in our human make-up - it lurks, waiting for an opportunity to express itself.

We are given the names of these 'wise' counselors that Ahasuerus has summoned to give him the advice that will soothe his ruffled passions.

Foolish Wisemen

Again, the names of these most trusted advisors are meaningful and give us the clues to how we are to understand what these 'wise men' represent and surmise the counsel each one offers. Their counsel may sound familiar to us and even make us squirm at how often we, too, call for these same 'wise men' to give us advice!

Following is the list and a description of the councilors Ahasuerus turned to.

Carshena - means 'a lamb, sleeping'. Oh, how important it is to us that we 'look' innocent, to prove it was not our fault. But our 'innocence' is sleeping, closing our eyes to our guilt does not make us guiltless - it just makes us feel better. There is a Latin phrase from Roman law that translated says "Ignorance of the law does not excuse." We also read an echo of that truth in Romans 1:20 ***"so then they are without excuse."***

Shethar - means 'putrefied, searching'. When we are trying to justify ourselves, we often search in 'putrefied' areas. We have Job's complaint recorded in Job 13:28 about how man decays like a rotten thing, there is nothing good in him. I Corinthians 1:20 addresses the foolishness of those who search for wisdom in this world, ***"Where is the wise? Where is the Scribe? Where is the disputer of this age? Has not God made foolish the wisdom of this world?"*** All advice contrary to the wisdom that is of God, is putrefied and will stink if we apply it to our lives.

Admatha - means 'cloud of death, or a mortal vapour'. Proverbs 16:25 speaks to Admatha and his cloud of death advice, ***"There is a way that seems right to a man but its end is the way of death."*** If it sounds right, if it feels good, we justify doing it - ignoring the fact that our feelings do not define the standard of right and wrong, good or evil - and death awaits at the end.

Tarshish - means 'greedy one'. How easily do we justify a desire with an argument from the point of 'need'? I need this … I need that … and we feel we are entitled to possess it. We do not heed the warning in Proverbs 1:19 that says, ***"So are the ways of everyone who is greedy for gain; it takes away the life of its owners."*** There is no room for contentment in those who follow this advice.

Meres - means 'dispute, quarrel'. When we are denied, how quickly we are discontented and grumble, and pick a quarrel. An angry heart will overflow and cause seeds of discord to spring up and choke out all peace and harmony. Jesus, in Luke 6:45, tells us that what we fill our heart with will come out of our mouth, ***"For out of the abundance of the heart, his mouth speaks."***

Marsena - means 'bitterness of a bramble'. How quickly bitterness finds a place to take root in an angry man or one who feels that an undeserved injustice has been done to him or he has been denied that which was his by right. Job put words to this emotional response in Job 10:1, ***"My soul loathes my life; I will give free course to my complaint, I will speak in the bitterness of my soul."***

Memucan - means 'impoverished to prepare certain truth'. When we begin with our own wisdom, how impoverished we are! There is no truth, or good, in us if we deny God's words of wisdom and trust in our own foolishness. ***"The fool has said in his heart, 'there is no God'. They are corrupt, and have done abominable iniquity. There is none who does good,"*** ~Psalm 53:1.

These advisors in our parable stand ready to offer their advice as soon as Ahasuerus should ask for it. Do we keep any of these counselors - so full of worldly self-interest - close to us, so that we can consult them quickly and easily when we need their advice and 'wisdom'?

Esther1:15-22

"Queen Vashti", the king said, "has failed to obey my royal command - the command of King Ahasuerus conveyed through the eunuchs! What does the law say should be done to her?" 16Memucan replied before the king and the officials, "Queen Vashti has done wrong

*not only to the king but also to all the officials and to all
the peoples in all of the king's provinces. 17The refusal
of the queen will be reported to all the women with the
result that it will make them despise their husbands.
They will say, 'King Ahasuerus commanded Queen
Vashti to be brought in before him, but she did not
come!' 18This very day the ladies of Persia and Media
who have heard of the refusal of the queen will tell it to
all the king's officials, and there will be contempt and
strife! 19If it seems best to the king, let him send out a
royal edict. Let it be written among the laws of Persia
and Media, never to be repealed, that Vashti may
never again come before King Ahasuerus. Let the king
give her place as queen to another who is more worthy
than she. 20When the king's decree which he makes is
heard throughout his kingdom — great as it is — the
wives of all classes will give honor to their husbands."
21The proposal pleased the king and the officials, and
the king did as Memucan advised. 22He sent letters to
all the provinces, to every province in its own system
of writing and to every people in their language, that
every man should be master in his own house!*

The Spokeman's Advice

Memucan steps forward as the spokesperson for Ahasuerus'
advisors. How fitting that is in light of his name meaning,
'impoverished to prepare truth'. The advice he offers is
designed to tickle Ahasuerus' ears yet, in the end, it will
impoverish him. Ahasuerus did not stop to reflect on the

fact that he was selective in his hearing, open only to the words that stoked his ego and confirmed his right to be vindicated for his humiliation.

The worldly counsel that we listen to, while it may be full of feel-good advice - all of it in the end is empty, impoverishing us while, at the same time, alluring us with promises that it will either enrich us or protect us from loss. While Ahasuerus' advisors were claiming their advice was meant to preserve Ahasuerus' control over his kingdom, in reality, their advice could only lead to discontent and loss.

In Malachi 1:4 we find the word 'impoverished' that we see in Memucan's name meaning. This passage speaks about Edom who turned against God, and God left them to follow their own ways. They eventually acknowledged their resulting **impoverishment** but arrogantly declared that they could simply rebuild. In no uncertain terms, God said 'no way!'.

Jesus speaks to the Revelation church who had turned to their own counselors, listening to and following their own inclinations, doing what served their own best interests. They looked so good on the outside, but He points out the blindness and impoverishment that comes with following worldly advice. Hear his words, ***"… you say 'I am rich, have become wealthy, and have need of nothing' –and do not know that you are wretched and miserable, poor, blind and naked,"*** ~Revelation 3:17.

From the beginning God warned of the impoverishment that comes when we indulge and lean on our own understanding.

"You shall not at all do as we are doing here today, every man doing whatever is right in his own eyes." ~Deuteronomy 12:8

"See, I have set before you ... life and good, death and evil ... I command you to keep His commandments ... But if your heart turns away so that you do not hear, and are drawn away ... I announce to you that you shall surely perish ... choose life that you and your descendants may live," ~ from Deuteronomy 30:15-20.

Rejecting His Queen

Even though Ahasuerus used all the excuses in the book to get what he wanted, his demand of his queen was not obeyed. Remember, earlier we concluded that while our will rules over our spirit, we cannot command it to perform contrary to the purpose that is God-ordained. I don't want to draw too deep an analogy to Ahasuerus' demand for his queen to expose herself in public, but I think we might do something of the same if we mock our spirit, deny that we are spiritual beings, or the other extreme where we try to dictate to our spirit to give us answers about spiritual, hidden things we do not know about. As God warns in Jeremiah 14:14, *"... The prophets prophesy lies in My*

name, I have not sent them, commended them, nor spoken to them, they prophesy to you a false vision, divination, a worthless thing, and the deceit of their heart." God will not speak to our spirits at the command of our 'will'.

While we cannot misuse our spirit, we can, however do what we see Ahasuers do to his queen, namely, reject our spirit in refusing to allow it to have any voice or influence in our lives. We want to rule, and we do not want anything to speak contrary to us nor do we want to be hindered or denied in anything that we set our minds to.

Our spirit has God's hand on it - by it He knows what we are about. He knows our every desire, He knows our every thought - and through our spirit He speaks to us. In Proverbs 20:27 we read, **"The spirit of man is the lamp of the Lord, searching all the inner depths of his heart."** And Job 32:8 says, **"But there is a spirit in man, and the breath of the Almighty gives him understanding."** If we reject our spirit, refusing to listen to God prompting us through it, preferring to go our own way, we turn our heart to stone. (Mark 3:5, Ezekiel 36:26)

It's My Right

Ahasuerus does not choose life. He refuses to consider the wisdom of his queen, in fact, does not even consider her well-being. He chooses to listen to the advice of those who have nothing good to offer, as we so naturally do likewise. It has been said, and is sadly true, that we learn more from our mistakes than from our successes, but if we were smart we would learn from the mistakes of others, saving ourselves the pain of repeating them. The truly wise man listens to, and obeys the words of God, thereby ensuring that he will have a good and successful life.

Ahasuerus is not, yet, a wise man and he listens to the words of his trusted advisors. He believes their warning that if he does not reject his queen he will lose more and more control over his kingdom. They encourage him to take a stand and defend his right to do as he wills. Of course, Ahasuerus follows their advice, rejects his queen, and banishes her from his sight. Now he can settle back to enjoy his new freedom. Notice the wording of verse 22, *"he sent letters to all the king's provinces, to each province in its own script, and to every people in their own language, that each man should be master in his own house, and speak in the language of his own people."* Note the 'to each his own' language in this verse … 'own script', 'own language', 'own house', 'language of his own people'. It corresponds to us saying to ourselves, "Whatever I feel, whatever I desire, whatever appeals to me, whatever I want … I give myself the right to have!" What extreme and complete self-indulgence! It is like the man that Jesus described in Luke 12:16, who planned his life of ease and God simply said, *"you fool…."*

Are we not often confronted by the same argument expressed by Memucan, that if we allow something once, there is no telling where it will lead? Maybe we are nudged to step out of our comfort zone to do a good deed, or donate to a worthy cause, and we are afraid of what it will cost us in the long run, or we hesitate to deny ourselves of some excess because we fear what others might say about us, or worse, that we will be impoverished.

Ahasuerus' wise men have only one measure for their wisdom - how does it serve or protect SELF.

CHAPTER FOUR

The Loneliness of Self

Esther 2:1

"Sometime later, when the wrath of King Ahasuerus had subsided, he remembered what Vashti had done and what had been decreed against her..."

Time Changes Things

"Some time later ...." Time has passed, though we are not told how much. Perhaps the amount of time is not important, rather, the focus is on what changed in Ahasuerus during that period of time.

The first thing we note is that the wrath of the king has subsided. Doesn't time do that to anger? Anger is hard to sustain over a long period of time. Often the original cause of the anger blurs in our memory - and in hindsight, we realize the issue wasn't as wrath-worthy as we deemed it to be.

When Ahasuerus' anger is finally dissipated, he finds

himself in a different kind of sober, and he remembers the good things about Vashti and the things he loved about her. He also remembers what he decreed against her. He feels the regret birthed by loneliness and discontent.

So often, in our anger, we decree destruction and chaos. When time passes and we recognize what we have lost, we find the damage we caused is irreparable; some things just can't be put back the way they were. The best case scenario is that something has been learned that will help us to be better in the future.

If Only

Another thing that happened with the passing of time is that Ahasuerus learned that living according to his own rules and desires did not bring him the happiness he expected it would. All of us have at some time or another played the 'if only' game, "If only I had a million dollars ... if only I had a new car, a bigger house, a better job, children, husband/wife ... if only I could lose twenty pounds ...." We make our 'if only' list but if we attain to anything on the list, we find it didn't satisfy us the way we had hoped, and we are left emptier and even more dissatisfied than we were. It is so true that our own way leads to death - death of peace, death of joy, death of fulfillment, death of love, and ultimately, even death of life. Insisting on our own way is a lonely existence; no one wants to keep company with us. There is a verse in Proverbs that speaks to this in contrast, ***"In the way of righteousness is life, and in its pathway there is no*** *death,"* ~Proverbs 12:28. In every path, except the one God has laid before us, there is only death at the end; every pursuit of happiness we eagerly follow - sooner or later - bursts like a bubble. In Proverbs 19:21, we read, *"There are many plans in a man's heart, nevertheless the Lord's counsel - that will stand."* This verse is a reminder that no matter how many plans man devises to grasp at success, in the end it is only the Lord's counsel that will prove true.

As we continue our story of Esther, we see that Ahasuerus is still looking in all the wrong places for his happiness. Let's read on .....

Esther 2:2-4

Then the king's servants who waited upon him said, "Let beautiful young virgins be sought for the king, 3and let the king appoint commissioners to all the provinces of his kingdom to gather them all to Susa the royal residence. Let them be brought into the women's quarters under the custody of Hegai, the king's eunuch, who has charge of the women. Then give them what is needed to make them beautiful, 4and let the girl who pleases the king be queen instead of Vashti." The proposal pleased the king so he put it into action.

Lonely Without Love

Ahasuerus, feeling lonely, sad, and dejected, searches his mind for something that would make him feel better. His trusted advisors, understanding him well, know that Ahasuerus loves wine, women, song, and endless feasting. In the time that has passed, Ahasuerus has probably had his fill of all of them, and the suggestion is quickly presented to him that it is a new queen that he needs. The idea meets with the expected approval of Ahasuerus, and he is filled with hope that he will feel happy again soon.

I find it interesting, that no matter how much the world tries to deny God, it cannot conceive of life without love. This fact is articulated in the familiar mantra, "Love makes the world go round". It is God who spun the world on its axis and put love into everything He created - because He IS love. Unable to deny his need for love, yet, deliberately denying his need for God, man has - throughout the ages - looked for love in all the wrong places. Our world today seems obsessed with every kind of immoral sex; a society so crazed for love that they have thrown caution to the wind and are looking to sex as though it is the answer they crave.

In our parable, Ahasuerus, as well, looked for love in the wrong places. Even, now, though he recognizes his need of a new queen, because he is king there is nothing restraining him in how he goes about it. His only consideration is for himself in his desire for all the beautiful, young virgins in his kingdom brought to his palace where he can enjoy them and make a choice at his leisure.

A Thankless Job

Hagai is the custodian of the king's harem that is housed in the women's quarters of the palace. His name means 'grieving, separation'. How fitting his name is, considering what a woman's lot is if she is forced to join the king's harem. It is a life of grief - grieving the separation not only from family, but also from her dreams. A young virgin brought into the king's harem would be brought to the king once, then never again unless the king calls for her by name. Though forgotten by the king, she is given a life sentence of being confined to the harem quarters and is never allowed to marry. Thus, the women placed in the care of Hagai, would understandably be grieving the death of their girlish dreams of one day having their own home, husband, children and grandchildren. It does not take much imagination to infer that the custodian of these women would have to hear their lamenting day in and day out. Not a happy job caring for these unhappy girls.

How easy it is to look at our lot in life and grieve. We grieve lost opportunities and life dreams that have eluded us. Perhaps we look at the wreckage of our life and lament that life is no longer worth living. We hate our life limitations and wish we had the privileges, the money, the beauty, the life style, the giftings, or talents of someone else. We grieve over the situations and circumstances that fill our life with suffering and hopelessness. We are so focused on the things that cause us pain and grief, that we miss the door God has opened to take us through. Too often, we waste time wishing for what we don't have, or what can never be, and are never thankful for what we do have. Our soul is cast down, and if we entertain the kind of thoughts and emotions that lock us into bitterness and discontent, the resulting despair will spread throughout our body until we feel we are little more than custodians of misery and unhappiness.

"Anxiety in the heart of man causes depression, but a good word makes it glad," ~Proverbs 12:25. Ahasuerus does not yet have the 'good word' that will make him glad.

CHAPTER FIVE

A Different Kind of Character

Esther 2:5-8

In Susa, the royal residence, lived a Jew named Mordecai. He was son of Jair, son of Shimei, son of Kish, a Benjamite. 6(Kish had been carried away from Jerusalem with the exiles who were deported with Jeconiah king of Judah, whom Nebuchadnezzar the king of Babylon took captive.) 7Mordecai had adopted Hadassah, that is, Esther, his uncle's daughter, since she had neither father nor mother. The girl was shapely and beautiful; and after her father and mother died, Mordecai raised her as if she was his own daughter. 8When the king's command and decree were known, many girls were gathered together to Susa the capital under the custody of Hegai. Esther was also taken into the king's palace and placed under the custody of Hegai, who had charge of the women.

We are introduced to another main character whose name is Mordecai. The first interesting detail given is that he is a Jew. That is significant since it immediately sets him apart from the other characters, who are all identified as Medes and Persians. So we know Mordecai is 'different'. Let us examine what we are told about him to determine who he represents.

Mordecai's Genealogy

We are given Mordecai's line of ancestry, a clue that we need to examine the meanings of the names of his father, his grandfather, and great grandfather, as well as the tribe the family belonged to.

Jair, the name of his father, means, 'my light, one who diffuses light'.

Shimei, the name of his grandfather, means, 'to perceive a sound, to hear, an observant listener, to obey'.

Benjamite, one who comes from the tribe of Benjamin, and Benjamin means 'son of my right hand'.

Putting these meanings together reveals that they are descriptive of the Holy Spirit.

- God diffuses His light throughout the world through the Holy Spirit. (Isaiah 9:2, I John 1:5, John 3:19)
- The Holy Spirit hears and speaks the word of God to man. (John 16:13)
- The Holy Spirit is spoken of as the Spirit of Jesus - Jesus who is the Son of the Right Hand of the power of God. (Luke 22:69, Ps. 89:17)

The Holy Spirit spreads the light of God, listens to and hears the word of God, then speaks it to man; he is the Spirit of the Father, and the Spirit of the Son. (Matthew 10:20, Philippians 1:19) We can already see that Mordecai, in our parable, represents the Holy Spirit, but there is more evidence to examine.

A Fishing Lure

There is one name we have not looked at - Kish, the father of Shimei, I know this may only be true in English, but Kish rhymes with fish, which fits with the meaning of Kish. Kish means 'to entrap by enticement, to lure'. Sounds like something a fisherman would relate to, doesn't it? Forgive me, if I am stretching the applied meaning somewhat, but has God not from the beginning sought to woo (entice) man to Himself? Did Jesus not instruct His disciples to do the same? ***"I will make you fishers of men,"*** -Matthew 4:19. Fishermen entrap by enticement. They dangle a lure in the water hoping some fish will take the bait. While being caught by a fishermen's hook is death, being caught by God's hook is life. We have the scripture that describes the 'lure' of God in John 12:32 where Jesus says, ***"And I, if I am lifted up from the earth, will draw all peoples to Myself"***, and we also have the work of the Holy Spirit described, in terms of luring men to recognize their need of God, in John 16:8-***11 "And when He has come He will convict the world of sin, and of righteousness, and of judgment, of sin because they do not believe in Me, of righteousness because I go to My Father and you see me*** *no more, of judgment because the ruler of this world is judged."*

Strong on our Behalf

The above passage, John 16:8-11, is a description fitting the actions of Mordecai in our parable as he exposes wickedness while he guards Esther and her people from harm. We see further parallel insight when we consider that the meaning of 'Mordecai' is, 'strong, able to crush'. The Holy Spirit of God, whose strength defends and empowers God's children, (Acts 1:8) is also able to crush the enemy on their behalf. (Romans 16:20)

Sweet Incense of Prayer

Furthermore, if we look at the Aramaic form of the name Mordecai, we find the added meaning of 'pure myrrh'. Myrrh is the aromatic resin used in incense, which pictures the fragrant scent of our prayers as they rise before God's throne. We read in Revelation 5:8, **"…and golden bowls of incense, which are the prayers of the saints."** We are also told that it is the Holy Spirit who helps us to pray, as we read in Romans 8:26, 27, **"Likewise the Spirit also helps in our weaknesses. For we do not know what we should pray for as we ought, but the Spirit Himself makes intercession for us…."**

Ever Present, but Ignored

In the details given regarding Mordecai, we note that he is in the palace. Though he is present, we see no indication that he is even noticed. He is totally ignored by the king and all his revelers and servants. But is that not often true of the Holy Spirit as well? God fills the universe, there is nowhere that He is not. He is omnipresent - ever present - but so often ignored, sadly, even in the hearts and lives of those who call themselves His children and claim to have His indwelling presence. But ... we are getting ahead of ourselves.

Introduction of Esther

Along with the introduction of Mordecai onto the stage of our parable, we are also introduced to another character - Hadassah, or Esther. We are told she is Mordecai's cousin and was raised by him after her parents died. Since she is related to Mordecai, we know that Esther, too, is a Jew.

So who is Hadassah, or Esther? Again, first clues lie in the name meaning. Hadassah is a Hebrew name which means myrtle. The myrtle was a white flower used for perfume. Here, we see a connective characteristic between her and Mordecai. Both of their names have to do with fragrance. However, we know Hadassah by the Persian form of her name, which is Esther. The Persian meaning of the name Esther is 'hidden'. While a modern meaning attributed to Esther is 'star', we can still see the original meaning. Stars are only seen at night; during the day they are hidden from view.

Esther represents our spirit. "But wait," you object, "wasn't Vashti our spirit?" Yes, but I believe the parable uses two women to depict our spirit because the Bible speaks of two. Look at Ezekiel 18:31, ***"Cast away from you all the transgressions which you have committed, and get yourselves a new heart and a new spirit, for why should you die ...."*** Note the wording, **"get yourselves a new spirit"**. Ahasuerus has had a change of heart, and he is getting himself a new queen - not restoring the old one. God also commands us to get a new spirit - one that will be sensitive to Him.

Filling the Spiritual Void

Ahasuerus is not going out to seek the one who will be his queen, rather he is having many virgins gathered together in his palace. Presumably, he will take his time to choose the one he desires most. What can we possibly understand this to mean?

Man has always recognized within himself a need to worship, the need to be spiritual, to have some expression of religious ritual. Man cannot deny that he is a spiritual being. So like all men, who try to deny their 'spirit', as Ahasuerus pictures in rejecting Vashti, they have to try to fill the emptiness that is left. There are many 'spirits', clothed with many religious cloaks, offering to fill that empty place. At this point in our story, Esther is only one of many being considered. We see that while Ahasuerus has awakened enough to recognize his need, he is not yet sure what exactly it is that he needs. In our own spiritual journey, God is always watching, wooing us, moving us - sometimes inch by inch - toward Himself, even as we explore other religious or spiritual paths. We follow first one, then another, of the many voices that cry out that they have what we are looking for to satisfy that hunger deep within us.

No one, in searching for fulfillment or meaning in life, can deny that God is there. No matter where any one goes, God, by His Spirit, is not only within reach but is reaching out to reveal Himself. Paul, in Romans 1:19, 20, speaks to this, pointing out that man is without excuse because the very creation of nature around him proclaims the character of God. He is always waiting and willing to give His Spirit to anyone who asks of Him. (Luke 11:13)

In looking back to our parable we have concluded that Esther is related to Mordecai, and she is one of the lovely virgins snatched from her home and taken to Ahasuerus' palace.

The Beauty Preparation

The women taken to the king's palace and joined to his harem were given a yearlong 'complete beauty treatment' that our modern spas would love to be able to offer. I don't want to take this too far in symbolism, but I think we could agree that there is a preparation that happens in our lives before we come to that place of getting a new spirit. I know in my own life, I can, in hindsight, point to many influences - be it people, circumstance, books, experiences - that turned my heart toward God, softened it and brought a new fragrance into my heart attitude and understanding. Remember in the verse quoted above, God said, ***"get you a new heart, and a new spirit"***. The new heart is important too, it cannot be the old hardened heart - it must be a new one of flesh, made soft, fragrant and sensitive, ready to receive and dwell with a new spirit.

Esther 2:9

The girl pleased him (Hegai) *and gained his favor, so that he quickly gave her the cosmetics she needed to enhance her beauty and her allowance of food and the seven maids selected from the king's household. He also transferred her and her maids to the best place in the harem.*

Standing Out Above the Crowd

When Esther was placed, along with the other women, under the care of Hegai, it did not take long for Esther to stand out, and we read that she pleased Hegai. Since we know Hegai was a eunuch, we know it was not her physical beauty that attracted him to her. It was something deeper that made her different from the other women. We are not told what it was that gave her favor in his sight, but following our analogy the meaning is easy to appreciate. The spirits of all false religion paths are in error and deception. Truth needs no defense. It stands alone above the crowd and always draws attention, stirring in people an emotional reaction that causes them to either accept it with joy, or reject it in anger. Something about Esther projected truth and purity - how could it be otherwise, since she was raised by Mordecai.

Esther could have grieved with the other women of the harem, believing her life to be over, yet, God had a plan for her, and she clung to what she had learned from Mordecai and continued to trust him.

God is able to take the unexpected twists and turns of our lives and weave all the detours and dead ends into something beautiful. The secret is to believe that every detail of our life is important to God and has a purpose. Only as we keep our eyes on the Lord and our trust unwavering in Him, with our fear and anxiety melted in His love and our sense of purpose rooted in His will, will we stand strong, our head held high, no matter what life storms we face. We have God's promise, *"And we know that all things work together for good to those who love God, to those who are the called according to His purpose,"* -Romans 8:28.

Esther 2:10

Esther had not revealed her people, nor her family background, because Mordecai had ordered her not to. 11Every day Mordecai would walk in front of the courtyard of the harem and ask after Esther's health and what was happening to her. 12The girls were prepared for meeting King Ahasuerus for twelve months: six months being treated with oil of myrrh and six months with perfumes and cosmetics. After the twelve months, 13each girl went in to the king. She was allowed to take with her whatever she wished from the women's quarters, 14and would enter the palace in the evening and return the next morning to another part of the harem under the care of the king's eunuch Shaashgaz who was in charge of concubines. She would not go to the king again unless he desired her and summoned her by name.

Esther has not yet revealed her people or kindred. We see how Esther takes all her cues and direction from Mordecai - there is a close and precious relationship between them. He watches over her so carefully, full of concern for her well-being.

Did you catch the reference to Esther's six months of preparation with the oil of myrrh? We saw the meaning of 'pure myrrh' in Mordecai's name and considering our scripture connection to myrrh and prayer, could we make the analogy stretch to include the importance of prayer to facilitate changed lives?

Entertained for a Night

We cannot help but recoil at the thought of the women gathered together in Ahasuerus' palace, where each one takes her turn to go to him for a night. But if we lift our eyes from the story to the parable application we know that is how that works in our own experience. In looking for the meaning of life, we hear of a philosophy that catches our attention, and if it stirs us deep enough it even keeps us awake at night. Lying on our beds, we follow our thoughts, considering and examining the new concept or perspective. If in the morning, we find our conclusions unacceptable, we turn away from the 'virgin idea' and consider it no longer. At best, we may tuck it into the back of our mind to pull out for some future reconsideration. We then look for the next fad or world view or spiritual path to intrigue us for a time, hoping that this time it will fill that inner void. In the end, everything disappoints and nothing lasts.

CHAPTER SIX

Choosing A New Queen

Esther 2:15-18

When it was the turn of Esther (the girl adopted by Mordecai, daughter of his uncle Abihail) to go in to the king, she only took with her those things that Hegai, the king's eunuch in charge of the women, had advised her to take. Esther was liked by all who saw her. 16Esther was taken to King Ahasuerus in the royal palace in the tenth month, the month of Tebeth, in the seventh year of his reign. 17And the king loved her more than all the other women, and she became his favorite and won his affection. He placed the royal diadem on her head and made her queen instead of Vashti. 18Then the king gave a great feast to all his officials and courtiers in honor of Esther, and he remitted the taxes of the provinces and distributed gifts with royal liberality.

Esther came to the king in the month of Tebeth. Tebeth means 'rain'. The Jews had a saying that if Tebeth was rainy, there would be a good harvest. Again, not wanting to take the analogy too far, I think because the month is named it must have some importance to add. If we take Jesus' parable of the sower and the seed, we know the seed that falls on fertile, well watered soil will grow and yield much fruit. And so we see in our parable, that the night Esther comes to Ahasuerus is the beginning of change - hopefully, a harvest of goodness in Ahasuerus' life and kingdom.

Falling in Love

Ahasuerus falls in love with Esther, and he loves her more than all the rest of the women. He offers her the ultimate honor and makes her his queen. Now, with a queen at his side once again, he can be fruitful in begetting children. Only through his rightful heirs can a king's dynasty continue through his family line after his own death.

Looking in the parable mirror, we understand this to picture what happens when we are born again. We have a new spirit and a new heart. We now have the hope of eternal life - we will continue to live beyond this earthly life, death is no longer something to fear. It is simply the threshold that we step over into a glorious eternity where we will reap the rewards of a fruitful earthly life. We begin our eternal kingdom life when we receive a new heart and spirit, when we see Jesus and fall in love with Him! We are changed!

What is Ahasuerus' response to having a new queen? He does what he does so well; he gives a feast! He announces a time of rejoicing, the forgiveness of taxes, and the giving of gifts to his subjects out of the generosity of his overflowing heart!

We remember our own conversion experience every time we see the joy of someone who has just been 'born again'. We remember "the grass is greener, the sky is bluer" kind of reaction and the desire to celebrate, to rejoice in our new found freedom and forgiveness. We want to permeate our being with the goodness of the new life that we have received. " … *[Jesus] whom having not seen, you love. Though now you do not see Him, yet believing, you rejoice with joy inexpressible and full of glory,*" ~I Peter 1:8.

We even find a parallel to the 'forgiving of taxes' that we see pictured in our parable. What is Colossians 2:13, 14 talking about if not the forgiveness of 'taxes' owed? *"….having forgiven you all trespasses having wiped out the handwriting of requirements that was against us, which was contrary to us. And He has taken it out of the way, having nailed it to the cross."* When we are born again, we are no longer burdened with guilt over debt (taxes) owing.

CHAPTER SEVEN

The Plot

Esther 2:19-23

At the time the virgins were assembled again, Mordecai was sitting as an official at the king's gate. 20Esther had not revealed her people or family background because she still obeyed him as she had when he was bringing her up. 21In those days while Mordecai was sitting in the king's gate, two of the royal court attendants, Bigthan and Teresh, who guarded the entrance of the palace, became enraged and attempted to kill King Ahasuerus. 22But Mordecai learned of the conspiracy and disclosed it to Queen Esther, and she told the king on Mordecai's behalf. 23When the affair was investigated and the facts discovered, the conspirators were both hanged on the gallows. The incident was recorded in the presence of the king in the daily record of events.

There is so much packed into those few verses.

Let's enjoy unpacking them and assigning the spiritual analogies.

Having our Cake and Eating it too!

The first part ... *"when virgins were gathered together a second time,"* seems confusing. Esther has been chosen, she has been made queen ... why is there to be a second gathering of virgins? Even in Israel's journals of their kings, we see the same pattern of plural wives and multiple concubines. It seems the one-man-one-wife did not apply to kings, not in Israel nor the heathen nations. So perhaps we should not be surprised to see that the virgins are gathered again in Ahazuerus' palace. I think we can, however, see how neatly this fits into our parable picture.

When we are born again, our spiritual understanding is opened and we 'see' with new eyes. We begin to be aware of things in our life that need to be changed, but we do not mature overnight, it is a process. At first we have one foot in the kingdom, while one foot is still lagging behind in the world. We are spiritual and yet still carnal. And we see this carnality portrayed in Ahasuerus, who, having made a good beginning in choosing his new queen, sees no reason to turn away from all others. Isn't it our temptation as well, to want to live in both worlds, to have our cake and eat it too? It takes time and discipline to become mature and Christ like. We begin as babes and must grow, as we read in I Peter 2:2, *"as new born babes, desire the pure milk of the word that you may grow thereby"*. While we are clean and forgiven, the habits and traits that cling to us do not automatically fall off to give way to better, and godlier characteristics and life habits. From who we were, to what we shall be, is what is called the sanctifying process.

As long as we are serving Self, we are not aware of any conflict, but when we are born again, suddenly, we find ourselves in a battle. And thus we shall see it unfold in our parable. Ahasuerus is 'born again', but there is trouble brewing in his kingdom.

The Doorkeepers

The curtain is being lifted in our parable to picture the spiritual reality in a new believer's life. We see that, even though Esther has been crowned queen, she is still listening to, and obeying, Mordecai. Their relationship is close. While she has not yet revealed who 'her people' are, we know that her people are Mordecai and the rest of the Jews in the kingdom. They represent the things of the Holy Spirit, everything that is godly, everything pertaining to God and His ways.

While we expect good things in the kingdom with Mordecai and Esther rising in prominence, not everyone in the kingdom is happy about the change. Ahasuerus and Esther are blissfully unaware, but there is intrigue being carried on behind the scenes. While the evil is veiled in secrecy, there is one who is watching, namely, Mordecai, who sees and knows all. He informs Esther of the plot details, and instructs her to warn Ahasuerus that his life is in danger. The guilty pair are none other than the king's two door keepers, Bigthan and Teresh. These two, we are told, became furious and sought to lay hands on Ahasuerus. What so infuriated them, we are not told, probably, because they needed no other reason than the fact that the king had a new queen.

What do doorkeepers do? They guard the house, they decide who comes in and who is forbidden entry. Our home doorkeepers, today, are locks and alarm systems. But for Azasuerus' there was Bigthan and Tesesh. We have established that our parable has to do with the kingdom of our physical being, so then can we identify our 'doorkeepers'?

We take our physical bodies so for granted, that there is much we just never think about. But consider this - imagine you did not have your five senses. Imagine that you are blind; now imagine that you are not only blind but also deaf; now imagine that you are not only blind and deaf but also have no sense of touch or taste, and you have lost your sense of smell as well. Do you not feel like all the lights have gone out of your kingdom and it has become very small, isolated and claustrophobic? Do you not have a sudden sense of wanting to scream to escape its narrow confines of complete darkness and its total … silence?

We don't stop to think that only what comes in and out of our palace doors, provides the means by which we are able to connect with and be aware of anything outside our inner self. We need our senses, they are the only way we can communicate with anything outside our body.

Without our 'doorkeepers', we have no way of gaining any information and would, in fact, be so isolated that we would be disconnected from everything we need for life and well-being.

So, then, who are the two doorkeepers named Bigthan and Teresh? We have learned by now to look at their name meanings for a clue. Bigthan means 'gift of God', and Teresh means 'desire'. The meanings sound like good things, and so they are. Having defined doorkeepers as the sentinels that control incoming information, we then easily recognize the parable interpretation to be that it is our eyes and our ears that stand guard at the 'doors' of our mind. But how do Bigthan and Teresh's name meanings fit into this? We note how, in I John 2:16, there is a connection between desire and the eyes - ***"the lust*** [or desire] ***of the eyes"*** - and, therefore we can see the aptness of Teresh's name meaning. If Teresh represents our eyes, then logically, Bigthan must represent our ears. Our hearing is truly a gift of God, as his name meaning states, but do we always use our ears to listen to only the things that honor God? It is a bit jarring to think of a 'gift of God' being used to plot against us, but is it not true? To use a gift in a way that dishonors the gift-giver, is the ultimate in disrespect and ungratefulness.

We absorb the world and all that is in it, primarily through our eyes and our ears. We choose what we will look at, enjoy, or lust after. We choose what we will hear, be it the things that honor God, or the things that are contrary to Him. We choose, blessing or cursing, by what we give permission to our 'doorkeepers' to allow into the palace of our mind. Some things are good and beautify our kingdom with life and light, but some things come with intent to harm or destroy. It is more serious than we are often willing to admit, and so we shall see it portrayed in our parable.

On Guard – Watchful

Except for the ever-watchful Mordecai, Ahasuerus would have been a hapless victim. Was he innocent? No, no more than we are - our doorkeepers are under our authority. We must instruct and train our doorkeepers as to what our self-determined standard is of what will be allowed to enter and what not. We see in our parable, when the king was informed of the danger, he took immediate action and had both Teresh and Begthan hanged – put to death.

Obviously, we can take the analogy too far and say the parallel here is that we should pluck out our eyes and cut off our ears … but wait, that sounds familiar, doesn't it? Didn't Jesus say something about it being better to pluck out an offending eye than for the whole body to be cast into hell? (Mark 9:47) David recognized the need for good doorkeepers when he said, in Psalm 101:3, *"I will set nothing wicked before my eyes."* We have the authority and power to 'put to death' those things that plot to harm us, those things that tempt us to allow wickedness to enter our doors through the things we watch and listen to. We could make our own list of things that we have allowed our doorkeepers to grant entry to, things that have not been good for us spiritually. Let us determine to follow Ahasuerus' example and 'put to death' the lax doorkeepers that are not a godly guard to protect us from harm.

In our parable, a record of this event regarding the doorkeepers, was made in the presence of the king. Do we not also record our experiences in the memories of our mind? This is not the last we will hear of this incident - but that comes later in our story.

While we are tempted and persecuted from without our kingdom, the real danger lurks within. In our own mind and body. The world has 'educated' us in such a way that we feel more comfortable with what the world offers than the new unfamiliar commandments by which we, as born again believers, are to govern our kingdom. It is only as we learn to understand and see the contrariness of the flesh against the spirit that we will find the peace and joy that is in Christ Jesus. Paul addresses this struggle in Romans 7 and then declares where the victory is to be found, ***"in Christ Jesus for those who do not walk according to the desires of the flesh but according to the Spirit."*** -Romans 8:1. We will learn more of this struggle in the next parable puzzle piece.

CHAPTER EIGHT

Here Comes Haman – Friend or Foe?

Esther 3:1-6

After these events King Ahasuerus promoted Haman the son of Hammedatha the Agagite, and advanced him to a place above all the officials who were with him. 2All the king's courtiers who were in the king's gate used to bow down before Haman, for so the king had commanded, but Mordecai did not bow down nor prostrate himself. 3Then the king's courtiers, who were in the king's gate, said to Mordecai, "Why do you disobey the king's command?" 4When they had spoken to him day after day without his listening to them, they informed Haman, to see whether Mordecai's acts would be tolerated, for he had told them that he was a Jew. 5When Haman saw that Mordecai did not bow down nor prostrate himself before him, he was furious. 6But it seemed to him beneath his dignity to

***lay hands on Mordecai alone, for they had told him
who Mordecai's people were. Instead Haman sought
to destroy all the people of Mordecai, all the Jews
throughout the kingdom of Ahasuerus.***

A new character walks onto parable stage. We feel an
immediate and instinctive dislike to this character. Who
is he? We are told that he is the son of Hammedatha. The
name Hammedatha means 'he that troubles the law'. A
very revealing meaning. If we define the law as the word
of God, then we easily recognize this character of Haman
for who he is. He represents what troubles us, what is
constantly working contrary to the word of God in our
life. Haman is none other than our flesh. (**Note** – *To
clarify the meaning of the word 'flesh' as it is used in this
book, it is not the flesh and bone of our physical bodies, but
it is used to refer to our 'old nature', the part of us that leans
toward the things of self, carnal, sin-bent and contrary to the
things of God.* e.g. Romans 5:8)

Perhaps some of you would suggest that he could also
be Satan. That sounds like a reasonable assumption until
we recognize that Haman is closely related to Ahasuerus
and has been elevated above all others who are WITH
Ahasuerus within the king's gate. Unless we are willing
to entertain the idea that we are all possessed with Satan,
to parallel Haman with Satan does not work. There are
more clues that will prevent us from assigning Satan to
the character of Haman, which we will see as our parable
unfolds.

Acting out a Name

The meaning of Haman's name has been lost to us, but we do have a clue as to what it could be. Since the Jewish celebration of Esther's story - the Feast of Purim - goes back thousands of years, it is reasonable to assume that they would have known the meaning of Haman's name. And, in fact, the meaning is still acted out in the yearly celebration. One of the traditions of the feast is that the scroll of Esther is read out loud. Whenever the name of Haman is about to be pronounced by the story-teller, the audience, pre-anticipating the name, will drown out the sound of 'Haman' with shouting or noise makers. So we could logically infer the meaning of his name to be 'multitude of noise'. Would that be descriptive of our flesh? When our flesh demands anything - be it comfort, food, gratification of any kind - and it is denied, is the reaction not a 'multitude of loud protests and noise'? All of us who are parents, have tried to hush a screaming baby in one arm as we hurry to warm the bottle with the other. Making a noise to get what we want is as natural to us as breathing! Unless we find a way to rule over the flesh, it will trouble us in ways we find hard to silence.

Haman's Family Tree

Another detail we are given, regarding Haman, is that he was an Agagite. Who are the Agagites? They are the descendants of Agag who we see in I Samuel 15. Agag was the king of the Amalekites. God instructed King Saul to go forth in battle against them and utterly destroy them all, both men and women, infant, child and all their animal herds. (*We will see the significance of this a little later in our parable.*) But Saul, in direct disobedience to God's command saved Agag alive, along with the best of the animals. When Samuel, the prophet, came to Saul and heard the bleating of the sheep and saw Agag was still alive, he demanded to know why Saul had not obeyed the voice of the Lord. Saul gives an interesting reply, insisting that he did obey, he killed all the Amalekites, mission accomplished as God had commanded him, and he even brags about bringing Agag back with him as a captive. But then, perhaps with a twinge of conscience, he points a finger of blame to the people, to justify himself. The people, he insisted, took the best of the plunder and the animals but only for the purpose of sacrificing them to the Lord. God's response to Saul is that the Lord does not have delight in sacrifices offered to Him that come out of disobedience, and He says, **"… for rebellion is as the sin of witchcraft and stubbornness is as iniquity and idolatry."** -I Samuel 15:21. Because Saul did not kill Agag as God had told him, God rejected him from being king. We know that Agag descended from Amalek, who was the grandson of Esau, and we know from Malachi 1:2-3 that God said the descendants of Esau would be **"a people against whom the Lord will have indignation forever."**

Never would an Amalekite or an Agagite find favor with God. Again we see how that speaks about our flesh. In Romans 8:1-10, Paul gives a sermon on how the flesh is contrary to the things of God and how those who walk according to the desires of the flesh are carnally minded and are at enmity with God. Verses 6-8 say, ***"For to be carnally minded is death, but to be spiritually minded is life and peace. Because the carnal mind is enmity against God, for it is not subject to the law of God, nor indeed can be, so then, those who are in the flesh cannot please God."***

Note the words 'is not subject to the law of God' and remember who the father of Haman was - Hammedatha, meaning, "he that troubles the law". So we see convincing evidence that, in the parable, Haman represents our flesh.

At Enmity

As our parable unfolds, we see that, when Mordecai enters the scene, Haman immediately sets himself against him. He does not just dislike Mordecai; he is filled with wrath against him. Wrath is never content to sit and stew in a corner, it must be acted upon and it seeks occasion to do so. Haman's people watch Mordecai and note that Mordecai does not honor Haman, who has been given a place of eminence by the king. While others bow and pay homage to Haman as he passes by, Mordecai ignores him. They are quick to point this out to Haman, then wait to see what Haman will do. We are told that Haman's wrathful revenge is directed, not only at Mordecai, but also against all his people who live in Ahasuerus' kingdom.

As we look at the enmity between Mordecai and Haman and apply the analogy to consider the same enmity between the Spirit and our flesh, questions arise in our mind. How intensely does the flesh hate the work of God in our life? Does it really rebel against God with intent to discredit Him? Does this picture really paint an accurate God-perspective of the destructive nature of our flesh? We hope that perhaps it is an exaggeration, but we have a disturbing confirmation explained in Galatians 4:28, 29, *(interestingly referring to Ishmael, whose nephew was Esau)* ***"But he who was born according to the flesh then persecuted him who was born according to the Spirit, even so it is now."*** And again in Galatians 5:17, ***"For the flesh lusts against the Spirit and the Spirit against the flesh and these are contrary to one another..."***

So the enmity we see pictured between Haman and Mordecai and his people is clearly a picture that depicts the flesh as our 'enemy'. But we have not stopped to define who Mordecai's people are. They represent anything that is of God, anything that pertains to the things of God - any godly thoughts, actions, and characteristics. Anything that is of God is contrary to the flesh and hated by it.

Trusting the Ememy

Ahasuerus is the one who promoted Haman to that elevated place of importance in the kingdom, second only to himself. Unaware of how great a potential enemy Haman is, Ahasuerus trusts him and keeps him close. The fact that Ahasuerus exalts Haman is duly noted by all who are in Ahasuerus' kingdom, and Haman enjoys great popularity. As we hear the story, it is easy for us to frown at Ahasuerus and shake our heads, wondering how he can be so ignorant to trust someone so obviously untrustworthy, so treacherous. But before we condemn Ahasuerus too quickly, remember this parable is a mirror that is reflecting our own image - this parable has our own name on it. How aware are we of the danger of the flesh? Do we recognize how quickly it can turn against us in wrath, seeking to destroy the very things that give us life in the Spirit? How deviously we are tempted by the flesh, yet how easily we give in to it. The flesh rashly promises to provide for our every comfort, our happiness, and our prosperity. Following the desires of the flesh will surely fulfill all our dreams! We have become wise to the empty promises that abound in our political election campaigns, but have we become wise to the empty promises of our flesh?

How Powerful is Our Enemy - Exactly?

We can look at a Biblical example of how powerful an enemy our flesh can be. King David, the shepherd king, was chosen by God - a man after God's own heart, a man who was sensitive toward God, who had a soft and quickly repentant heart, who was the greatest king Israel ever had - what high praise is heaped upon this man. The strength of a hungry lion was not strong enough to destroy him. The powerful giant Goliath, who caused the whole of Israel's army to tremble with fear, could not destroy him. King Saul, with all his military might and no matter how hot his wrath against David burned, could not destroy him. Not one of these enemies who hated David and came against him seeking his death, could hurt him. But the wrath of one enemy brought him down, one enemy overcame him - that enemy was his flesh. He lusted, he took what was not his, committed adultery, then, committed murder to cover his sin. The consequences were felt throughout his kingdom and troubled him for the rest of his life.

Haman is no friend to Ahasuerus, and our flesh is no friend to us.

CHAPTER NINE

Relinquishing His Rule

Esther 3:7-11

In the first month (the month of Nisan) in the twelfth year of the reign of King Ahasuerus, Haman had 'pur' (which means 'lot') cast before him to determine the best day and best month for his actions. The lot fell on the thirteenth day of the twelfth month --- the month of Adar. 8So Haman said to King Ahasuerus, "There is a certain people scattered among the peoples in all the provinces of your kingdom, whose laws differ from those of every other and who do not keep the king's laws. Therefore it is not right for the king to tolerate them. 9If it seems best to the king, let an order be given to destroy them, and I will pay ten thousand silver coins into the royal treasury." 10So the king took off his signet ring from his hand and gave it to Haman son of Hammedatha the Agagite, the enemy of the Jews. 11"The money is yours," the king said to

***Haman, "and the people also to do with them as you
wish."***

The purpose of Haman casting the lot, was to appeal
to some nameless entity, or power, to indicate which day
would be the lucky day on which to carry out his evil plan
against Mordecai and his people. Casting lots, in and of
itself, is simply random chance and has no power to imbue
any special favor or influence on the day the lot falls on.
Obviously, Haman was trusting in empty vanity. But, we
have a scripture verse that overrules the thought that the
casting of lots is nothing more than random chance. In
Proverbs 16:33 it says, ***"The lot is cast into the lap, but
its every decision is from the Lord."***

Haman casts his lot in the first month of the year, but
the lot falls in the last month of the year, forcing him to
have to wait almost a whole year before he can carry out
his evil plan. If God determined the day on which the lot
fell, what was His purpose in causing the lot to fall on a
day as far as possible from the day the lot was cast? I'm
sure Haman seethed when he saw how long he would have
to wait to carry out his wicked deed.

The Dice - Random Chance or in God's Hand?

This small detail about Haman casting the lot is included
in our story because it has a powerful message. It pictures
God keeping a watchful eye on those who would plot
against us - even including our own flesh.

What good thing is accomplished by Haman being
hindered from immediately destroying the Jews? It gives

Mordecai and Esther time to develop a closer relationship with Ahasuerus – strengthening the bond between them. So too, God gives us time and opportunity to grow into a deeper relationship with Him, becoming more sensitive to hear Him in our spirit and growing stronger in Him.

God's purpose in choosing the 'day' of our testing, or in hindering an attack of the enemy, is to give us time to get ready. God knows our weaknesses, He knows how strong some temptations are, and He will not allow a temptation to come against us that we do not have not the strength to resist. So the old adage, "the devil made me do it", is not a valid excuse because if a temptation in the flesh comes, we can know that God has given us the time needed to strengthen ourselves in order to withstand it.

In I Corinthians 10:13 it says, ***"No temptation has overtaken you except such as is common to man, but God is faithful who will not allow you to be tempted beyond what you are able, but with the temptation will also make the way of escape, that you may be able to bear it."***

A Threat to the Friendship

Haman, still in close fellowship with Ahasuerus, warns him that there is a people dispersed throughout his kingdom. These people are dangerous because they are different, and they follow contrary laws from those that Ahasuerus has decreed and is comfortable with. It would not be good for Ahasuerus to allow them to remain, insinuating that they have the potential to ruin his kingdom. The best resolution, Haman cunningly suggests, is for Ahasuerus to sign a decree that they be destroyed. Haman warns Ahasuerus that these people are already scattered throughout the land.

The 'people' that Haman refers to in our parable, symbolize the things of God that we have allowed to enter our thoughts and our mind that have had an influence on us. The Lord's commandments that we obey, and His ways that we have learned to know and to follow, have the power to change who we are. As we grow in our faith we set a new course and have a new vision of purpose. Of course, the flesh naturally rejects these things for they threaten its own well-being, and it will make a strong appeal to our will to guard the comforts of our flesh!

Ahasuerus has changed since he has a new queen, and the people related to Mortecai and Esther, who are scattered throughout his kingdom, have been singled out for notice. When we become believers, we have God's light enter us and we are given the indwelling Holy Spirit, but the things of God are, at first, only scattered throughout our kingdom. Though we are increasingly aware of them, we are not yet mature in our faith walk and we have a mix in our kingdom. The old has not yet been completely put off, and the new not yet completely put on. (Ephesians 4:17-24) What Haman fears will happen, pictures what is true for every believer. If we continue, faithful and obedient to the laws of God instead of the laws of self, all the things in us that are contrary to a godly life are threatened!

One's Temptation is Another's Strength

Haman comes with such appealing words to Ahasuerus in presenting his plan of action - "if it please you". He also tempts him with the promises of riches. How often are these the two strongest appeals to us from our flesh - this will please you, and/or this will improve your financial situation, or enrich your life in some way. To Ahasuerus' credit, he refuses Haman's offer of money. We must note that Ahasuerus does not refuse the money because he is wise to the devious ways of Haman. We see that he naively agrees to all Haman wanted. So what is the significance of his refusal of the bribe? We are not all tempted by the same things. Ahasuerus does not need more money, he already has more riches than he knows what to do with. A millionaire might not be tempted to take the ten dollars offered to him for something he is already willing to do. Someone who hates the taste of alcohol would not be tempted to get drunk at a party, or the smartest kid in the class is not tempted to copy someone else's paper. We all have our own areas of weakness where our flesh can present temptations we struggle to resist, while temptations in other areas we may easily turn away from. There is no justification for pride in resisting a temptation that has no power to draw us in.

Tempted and Drawn Away

It is our self-preservation instinct to draw back from something that we know will be uncomfortable or painful, or threaten us in some way. And that is where temptation finds its strongest ploy, to keep from us the awareness of any possible negative repercussions. How easily we gloss over the fine print. Remember that when the tempter came to Eve, he promised her gain if she took of the fruit and loss if she did not. Eating of the fruit looked like a win/win for her. So temptation always comes with the enticement of 'good', while at the same time, hiding the fact that the promise is false and holds a dagger behind its cloak.

Ahasuerus is blind to Haman's dagger and trusts his advice that there are people in his kingdom that must be destroyed. The fact that Haman slyly points out, that they do not obey the king's laws, appeals to the king's ego. His automatic response is that, of course, he must punish anything in his kingdom that stands in disobedience to him. His word is law, and his command must be obeyed.

The Signet Ring Authority

We feel disappointed to see that Ahasuerus considers Haman's proposition to be of wise counsel and, therefore, accepts it. He, then, goes one step further by taking off his signet ring and giving it to Haman. Today, we no longer automatically recognize the significance of this action. In times past, a signet ring was a seal of authority, a man's signature. Every man's signet ring had a personal, engraved design so that when he pressed his ring into wax to stamp a document, a letter, or a decree, it set his seal of authority on it - and that seal was recognized by anyone looking at it. In this simple action of taking off his ring, Azasuerus gives his authority to another. When we choose to place ourselves under someone's authority we make ourselves a slave to the one we have submitted to, as we read in Romans 6:16, *"Do you not know that to whom you present yourselves slaves to obey, you are that one's slaves whom you obey, whether of sin to death, or of obedience to righteousness?"*

Ahasuerus, unwittingly, gives authority to his enemy. We see how oblivious Ahasuerus is to Haman's evil intentions when we read his words, *"The money and the people and the authority are yours, go and do what seems good to you!"*

We want to shake some sense into Azasuerus and wish someone would warn him not to give authority to Haman, not to be drawn in by his devious words … but wait … who's reflection do we see when we look into the mirror - is it not our own? How often do we pull back from what we know God wants us to do? We decide that it will be too hard, or too invasive to our comfortable life-style, or too contrary to all we consider to be reasonable. We, too, take off our 'signet ring' and give our authority to our flesh, saying in effect, "Go and do whatever FEELS good to you!" Do we feel the sting of Paul's criticism? *"… For those who live according to the flesh set their minds on the things of the flesh … so then, those who are in the flesh cannot please God,"* -Romans 8:5a, 8.

CHAPTER TEN

Irrevocable Decrees

Esther 3:12-15

And so, on the thirteenth day of the first month, the king's secretaries were summoned and as Haman instructed, an edict was issued to the king's satraps and provincial governors and the rulers of each of the peoples in their own script and their own language. The edict was written in the name of King Ahasuerus and sealed with his ring. 13Dispatches were sent by couriers to all the king's provinces, saying, "Destroy, kill, put an end to all the Jews, young and old, little children and women, on the thirteenth day of the twelfth month, and plunder their possessions." 14A copy of the edict was to be published as a decree in every province --- publically displayed so that everyone might be ready for that day. 15By command of the king the couriers raced off, and the edict was published in Susa itself. Then the king and Haman sat down to drink, but the city of Susa was in turmoil.

While Haman cast his lot in the first month of the year, the lot fell on the last month of the year. Haman does not, however, wait until the end of the year to begin to put into place the details of his plot.

We see that Haman is not one to waste time, and in the very month he cast the lot, he begins to finalize his plans for that fateful day. He calls in the king's scribes to write the decree, and he seals it with the king's authority that is now in his hand. Copies of the decree are sent out to all the satraps, governors, and officials – written in the script each one understands, and in everyone's language. What is decreed, with Ahasuerus' proxy permission, quickly spreads to the uttermost parts of his kingdom.

The Thought and the Copy

Until recent medical science research, we would miss the incredible interpretation of this publishing detail in our parable. I referred earlier to Dr. Caroline Leaf's study of the brain that proves how quickly a thought is 'published' throughout our body kingdom. We see this portrayed, in our parable, in how the whole kingdom was immediately informed of Haman's plan and the resulting fear and anxiety was pervasive. Many years ago God said, ***"As a man thinks in his heart, so is he!"*** ~ Proverbs 23:7. Do we not see this illustrated in our parable? As Ahasuerus 'willed' and thought, so it was felt throughout his kingdom.

I find these words, "a copy of the document was to be issued", so interesting. Dr. Caroline Leaf points out that, "The brain builds a double memory of the content of every thought, one on the left side of the brain and one on the right." (*Who Switched off My Brain*, pg.17) In other words, we make a copy of our thoughts, not unlike the backup files we store on our computer to protect against loss.

As It is Written, So Let it Be Done

While this detail is not expounded on in the book of Esther, there is a Persian law that is important to our understanding of the parable. From secular historical accounts, but also from Daniel 6:8-15, we know that the law of the Medes and Persians stated that a decree once written, could never be changed, nor revoked. So we can be sure of Haman's glee when he saw the decree written and stamped with the king's seal. He knew that it could not be annulled, the Jews' demise was decreed, and therefore was as good as done!

We can easily recognize the truth as we apply this to ourselves. Once a thought is 'thinked', it can never be 'unthinked'. Nor can the chemical reaction our thought immediately begins in our 'body kingdom' be undone - the thought has set the process in motion. Is all lost? No, mercifully, it is not, as we shall discover as we continue to work through our parable.

A Kingdom Does Not Fall in a Day

There is significant meaning in the fact that the decreed destruction was planned and laid in place a year before the actual day the event would take place.

How true this plays out in our own life. Our actual 'fall' may be in a moment, in a day, but the preparation work to make that 'moment- in-time-destruction' possible was begun long before. We don't need anyone to tell us how a thought can grow in our minds until it keeps us awake at night. We all know the power a well-fed thought has to stir up our emotions and fuel our motivation to act or react. Finally, all our energy is focused on and consumed in the unavoidable consequences perpetrated by that first unbridled thought.

Scripture shows us the progression in James 1:14-15, ***"But each one is tempted when he is drawn away by his own desires and enticed. Then, when desire has conceived, it gives birth to sin and sin, when it is full-grown, brings forth death."***

Once the decree is written and the copies made, the dispersion of them is hastened by the king's command. His command must be obeyed; his will cannot be challenged. In the same way, if a negative, or sinful, thought is released with our consenting authority, it goes out with power to cause our body to comply with the thought's intent. Not only is our physical health affected but also our emotional, mental and spiritual condition. Ultimately, our resulting actions and reactions will cause our downfall.

We see this 'preparation-for-destruction path' so

clearly expounded by Paul in the first chapter of Romans. He tells us the first step on the road to spiritual destruction is being unthankful, as he points out in verse 21. Then follows a long list of progressively more revolting sins of the flesh until finally the day of destruction comes and it delivers … death. (Romans 1:32)

Closing our Eyes to the Obvious

This part of our parable ends with these words, ***"So the king and Haman, sat down to drink, but the city of Shushan was in turmoil."*** We readily understand why the king and Haman would sit down for a drink. It is not unlike any two businessmen, who have successfully completed a deal, and then they celebrate their signed agreement with a drink. So we see Haman and Ahasuerus comfortable with each other, sitting back, pleased with the partnership they have just forged. But the city (or kingdom) of Shushan is confused and in turmoil.

So often we set off a chain of reactions throughout our 'kingdom', oblivious to the havoc we are creating, until it is too late. We sit content, thinking we have all under control - yet the confusion in our body has begun. What exactly is meant by this descriptive Hebrew word translated into our English 'perplexed' or 'turmoil'? If we look at another place where this same Hebrew word is used, we can glean a better grasp of its meaning. In Joel 1:18, we read, ***"How the beasts groan! The herds of cattle are restless, because they have no pasture. Even the flocks of sheep suffer your punishment."*** The Hebrew word translated 'perplexed' in Esther, is translated 'restless' here in Joel, but what the context reveals is enlightening. Why are the cattle so restless or perplexed that they are groaning? Because they have no pasture. The order of their life has been upset, destroyed. If there is no pasture, they don't know what to do. Without pasture, everything important to the cattle's well-being is threatened; they have lost their sense of security, the order of their life is in chaos, and their life itself is threatened.

This is really a good picture of what is happening in Ahasuerus' kingdom. The people's sense of security is threatened, they do not know who is safe and who is not. Who will the king protect and who will be destroyed? There is nowhere to hide; the decree has been written.

That is also the reality of our 'kingdom' when we go against the order that God has established for our well-being. For example - God commands us to forgive, but if we don't forgive we are **"delivered to the torturers"**, ~Matthew 18:21-35. Unforgiving thoughts send distress, or trouble, throughout our body. According to the study of Worthington et al. (1999), they suggest that "unforgiveness can be viewed as a state in which a person is confined in a stressful state of mind." To go contrary to God's order and follow our own willful ways, is to upset our 'kingdom' into chaos, putting our health and life into danger. We sit in our smug resolve, but our 'kingdom' is in turmoil.

CHAPTER ELEVEN

The Picture of Grief

Esther 4:1-3

When Mordecai learned all that had been done, he tore his clothes and put on sackcloth and strewed ashes on his head, and went out into the city and raised a loud and bitter cry of lamentation. 2He went as far as the king's gate, but no one could enter the gate clothed with sackcloth. 3In every province, wherever the king's command and decree went, there was great mourning, fasting, weeping, and wailing among the Jews. Many of them sat in sackcloth and ashes.

My adult daughter came to me one day and said, "You know, Mom, I remember the day when I suddenly - to my utter shock - realized that I could hurt your feelings. Before that I just never had any concept of that being possible." I think we can all relate to that aspect of childhood. Our appreciation for our parents' feelings comes only with maturity. What we don't recognize is how often, and sadly, for how long, we have that same immature attitude toward God.

The Hebrew word translated into our English word 'grief' has all of the following words in its meaning: worry, pain, displeasure, grieve, hurt, be sorry. We understand grief best when we see someone suffering deep, agonizing sorrow for the loss of a loved one. But when we read the word 'grief' in reference to God, we somehow leave off the emotion. It is just too difficult to grasp that an infinite, all-sufficient Being, so 'other' compared to our insignificant self, could be in grief over us. So we tuck the word grief in our mental dictionary under the word angry. An angry God we can relate to - most religions have a god that must be appeased. It is natural to assume a god has the characteristic of anger, since we learned from early childhood that we could make our parents angry. To acknowledge an angry God is much easier than trying to wrap our minds around the concept of God's profound grief on our behalf.

But now, in our parable, we see Mordecai deep in a state of grief. We cannot look away; we cannot misinterpret it as anger. Mordecai is picturing for us the grief of the Spirit of God when He sees us turning away from where we are safe, and putting ourselves into a situation where we can be hurt or destroyed - where the consequences of our actions will cause pain and trouble in our kingdom.

We are disconcerted when we read the description of Mordecai's grief and realize that we are looking at a picture of God's grief when we hurt Him.

Mordecai at the Gate – Jesus Knocking on the Door

Mordechai, deep in grief and clothed in sackcloth, sits just outside the gate. No one is allowed to enter the king's citadel clothed in sackcloth, so Mordecai is as close as he can come, at the gate. Does this remind you of another scripture? How about Revelation 3:20, ***"Behold, I stand at the door and knock If anyone hears my voice and opens the door, I will come in to him and dine with him and he with Me."*** These words of Jesus are directed to the Laodiceans, who, just like Ahasuerus, had compromised the flesh until they were comfortable with it and did not know that, now, Jesus was outside the door, knocking, desiring to come back into fellowship with them. This parable picture showing Mordecai outside the gate, and the Revelation picture of Jesus outside the door, represent how effectively we can shut the Lord out of our thoughts and lives where we no longer pay any attention to Him at all. Our fellowship with Him is broken and He weeps, wanting us to turn away from the things that are distracting us and invite Him in, to once again dine together around a table of intimate fellowship.

The Cry of David when He Grieved the Spirit of God

We see how this played out in David's life in Psalm 51, written after he was rebuked by the prophet Nathan for his sin with Bathsheba. In verse 10, he says, ***"Create in me a clean heart, O God, and renew a steadfast spirit in me."*** He repented of the sin of his flesh and longed for a cleansed heart and a renewed spirit, one that was steadfast in single-mindedness. Then in verse 11 we read these words, ***"Do not cast me away from your presence, and do not take Your Holy Spirit from me."*** This is pictured so clearly with Mordecai at the gate. He is still there, he has not left - he is sitting, turned toward the king's gate, grieving. If we have a houseful of guests, we are quite content as long as they are in our house, but if one of them steps out the door, we say, "Oh! Are you leaving?" We feel the separation, we read the signs that they are going to leave. And so David, now aware of having broken fellowship with the Lord, cries out, "I want to be in your presence where I fellowship with you!" And he feels the conviction of the danger he has put himself into. He recognizes that because he has given in to the desires of the flesh, the Spirit is no longer comfortable abiding with him. And so he cries, ***"Do not take your Holy Spirit from me!"*** May that also be our heart cry if we feel we have broken fellowship with the Lord and shut Him out - may we quickly cry out for Him to come and surround us again with His presence and restore our fellowship with Him.

Grieving for our Children

Parents who have agonized over wayward children will hear God's expression of grief in Luke 13:34b, ***"... How often I wanted to gather your children together, as a hen gathers her brood under her wings, but you were not willing."***

We have examples in scripture of Jesus grieving. One, in John 13:21, where we read that Jesus, *"was troubled in spirit"*. Why? Because He saw that one of His own was going to betray Him. We have another example, in John 11:33, where it says about Jesus, *"He groaned in the spirit and was troubled."* Again, the reason was because He agonized, not for Himself, but for others, in this case, his friends who sorrowed over the loss of a loved one.

We are commanded in Ephesians 4:30, *"And grieve not the Holy Spirit."* The Greek word for 'grieve' is 'to distress, cause grief, be in heaviness, sorrow'. There is no mistaking the emotion meant here in using the word 'grieve'. Since a created thing, in and of itself, cannot grieve its creator, we know the reason we are told not to grieve Him is not because He is sensitive to being personally offended. He feels the profound grief because of us! It is the agony of a loving parent distressed over the harm and destruction their child is inflicting upon themselves. When we, as believers, listen to the ungodly demands of the flesh, we will feel the shadow of God's grief within us; we will feel the distress and turmoil of a divided heart that causes God to grieve and our kingdom to be troubled.

CHAPTER TWELVE

No Comfort for the Comforter

Esther 4:4-9

When Esther's maids and attendants told her about Mordecai's behavior, she was greatly troubled. She sent garments for Mordecai to put on, so that he could take off his sack-cloth, but he would not accept them. 5So Esther called Hathach, one of the king's eunuchs whom he had appointed to attend her, and ordered him to go to Mordecai to learn what it all meant and the reason for it. 6So Hathach went out to Mordecai, to the city square in front of the king's gate. 7Mordecai told him all that had happened to him and the exact amount of money that Haman had promised to pay into the king's treasury for the destruction of the Jews. 8Also he gave him a copy of the decree to destroy them, that had been published in Susa, to show to Esther for her information. He also told her to go to the king and implore his mercy and to plead with him in behalf of her people.

9 Hathach came and told Esther what Mordecai had said.

When we trouble our kingdom by indulging the flesh, our spirit is also troubled. Notice in our parable that Esther's communication with Mordecai is broken to the point that she does not know why Mordechai is in grief. Is that not one of the first things that happens when we are walking in the flesh, we pull away from our communing with the Lord? We close our Bibles and are suddenly too busy to pray. Like the child who has disobeyed, like Adam and Eve in the garden, our first instinct is to hide when we don't want to face God because we are still holding onto the pleasure of our sin.

Comforting Mordecai

When Esther hears about Mordecai's grief and that he is sitting outside the gate in sackcloth, she is understandably upset. Her first instinctive reaction is to comfort him - to take away his grief. We understand the feelings of compassion that flood over us when someone we love is hurt, suffering, or in grief. We desire to comfort them, to make the hurtful feelings go away, and so we mistakenly offer our comfort to God's Spirit if we recognize that He is grieved.

Years ago, I had a vision of Jesus after someone had wounded me, and I was emotionally distraught over it. In my vision, Jesus stood before me with deep, profound grief and compassion for me filling His eyes. My heart immediately reached out and my thoughts cried out,

"Ohh ... it's not that bad, please, please don't hurt so for me!" Even though I saw and felt the Lord's compassion for my pain, I was not allowed to justify my reaction toward the one who had hurt me. What the Lord desired was for me to let go of my hurt, give it to Him, and not sin in how I reacted to the offense committed against me. He did not want the offense to hold me in bondage.

So we see that Esther, recognizing Mordechai's grief, wants to comfort him by simply covering up his grief, but Mordecai refused her offering. Esther's comfort did not in any way address the *cause* of Mordecai's grief, only his expression of it. But there is another reason as well. When we reach out to comfort God - while we may mean well - we do not recognize that it is not our comforting gestures that He is looking for, but a change in our heart and behavior so that the cause of His grief will be taken away. To simply relieve emotion does not cure the wound. Covering the expression of grief, does not address the problem or provide any resolution. When we come to God, it must be in humility, and then it is He who comforts us - not the other way around. The roles cannot be reversed. His grief and His compassion toward us is meant to melt us and move us to obedience.

Esther accepts the rebuke of Mordecai, in his rejection of her offer, and she humbles herself to seek the cause of his grief. THAT is the response God looks for, is it not? A humble spirit that seeks restoration for the kingdom. Just as it is Esther who is the first to be aware of Mordecai's grief, so also our spirit is always first to recognize that something is wrong in the kingdom; that the relationship between us and God has been broken.

Where Is Ahasuerus?

In our picture showing Esther's distress over Mordecai's grief, we feel a nudge to wonder where Ahasuerus is that he is completely unaware that his queen is deeply troubled. We don't have to look far. Ahasuerus has been keeping company with Haman, ignoring the needs of Esther, not having called her in thirty days. Broken fellowship always results in distress of our spirit. In Luke 1:80, we read that John the Baptist *"grew and became strong in spirit."* John's life was centered on the things of God. We grow strong in spirit when we build ourselves up, spending time in God's word and in prayer - wanting more than anything else to be with Him. The stronger our spirit is, the more sensitive we will be to quickly hear and know if something is wrong. So the pictures holds true for us. If we ignore our spiritual needs and withdraw from spending time in communion with God, we will be unaware of lurking danger at our doorstep. The more we feed our spirit, the deeper our communion with God and the more sensitive we will be to His voice, warning us of the things that could harm us.

The Truth Always Holds the Answer

We are given the name of the servant that Esther sends out to make inquiries on her behalf as to the cause of

Mordecai's grief. His name is Hathach. While it is difficult to find meanings for ancient names, and not all sources even agree, I found it interesting that the only meaning I could find for the name Hathach is 'truth'. Which is, of course, exactly what Esther was seeking regarding what was wrong; she wanted the truth. Our spirit, in communion with the Holy Spirit, will always reveal to us what is true.

Hathach goes straight to the source, as everyone does who sincerely loves the truth; no time is wasted on hearsay or third party opinion. Hathach knows where he will find the truth - from Mordecai himself. And Mordecai is more than forthcoming; it seems he was waiting for Esther to inquire as to what is wrong.

Is there a lesson here? Is God also waiting for us to seek the truth from His mouth? We have a standing invitation, as James so clearly states, ***"If any of you lacks wisdom, let him ASK…"*** ~ James 1:5. I believe God often sits, waiting in vain, for us to come to inquire of Him. The passage just quoted goes on to promise that God will always answer the sincere seeker who comes with a plea for 'truth'. It says that God gives to all ***"… liberally and without reproach …"*** Here too, we see the generosity of God - He gives more than is asked for! How often do we stumble about in the darkness of our kingdom, seeking answers in all the wrong places, when all we have to do is ask for God's light?

Even in the Old Testament, we see God longing for, and waiting for, His people to inquire of Him. The whole of Isaiah 55 expresses such a heartfelt longing of God toward His children to come to Him for all they need or could wish for. God appearing to Solomon said, *"... Ask me ... what you want?"* ~I Kings 3:5. Read Psalm 2:8, Isaiah 45:1, Isaiah 7:11, Jeremiah 6:16, to see God repeat His heart-felt invitation, *"Ask me, ask me, ask me ... and I will give ...."*

Guarding our Inter-Spirit Connection

Looking into the mirror of our parable, we see that Mordecai tells Hathach everything that has happened and everything that is going on. Our inner being is not hidden to God, there is nothing he does not know about us, no detail escapes Him, and there is nothing He does not understand. In the beautiful words of Psalm 139, we read in verses 17-18, *"How precious also are Your thoughts to me, O God! How great is the sum of them! If I should count them, they would be more in number than the sand: When I awake, I am still with you!"* The picture that always come to my mind when I read this verse is one of God sitting beside my bed, watching me sleep and waiting for me to awake in the morning! To grieve the heart of a God so loving toward us in all His thoughts and ways, is almost inconceivable.

God in His love has *"the days fashioned for me"* (Psalm 139:16), so it is a given that He also is waiting to give us directions on how we should live our days. We see this in our parable as we listen to Mordecai give instructions to Esther as to what she is to do. Note that Mordecai does not request an audience before the king, nor does he suggest that Hathach go personally to the king and fill him in on what is going on. Mordecai gives instructions to be given to Esther. We need to treasure our spirit - it is not unlike the internet that we cannot live without today. If only we were as sensitive to a disconnect between our spirit and God's Spirit, as we are fearful of losing our internet connection.

We are beginning to see how Esther is the connecting link between Mordecai and Ahasuerus. Mordecai, who sees and knows everything that is going on, informs Esther who is then responsible for bringing an appeal to Ahasuerus. So it is with us as well. God, who sees and knows everything through His Holy Spirit, communicates to us through our spirit. In Romans 8:16 we read, ***"The Spirit Himself bears witness with our spirit that we are children of God."*** So we see in the 'bearing witness' of the Spirit of God with our spirit, the communication between God's Spirit and ours. Through our spirit, then, we are able to experience the Spirit of God, sensing His presence and His peace, and hearing His still, small voice.

CHAPTER THIRTEEN

For Such a Time as This

Esther 4:10-17

She (Esther) instructed Hathach to go and say to Mordecai, 11"All the king's courtiers and the people of the king's provinces know that for every man or woman who goes to the king into the inner court without being called there is one penalty, death, unless the king holds out the golden scepter signifying that they may live. It has been thirty days since I have been called to go in to the king." 12When Mordecai was told what Esther had said, 13he sent back this reply to Esther, "Don't imagine that you alone of all the Jews will escape because you belong to the king's household. 14If you persist in remaining silent at this time, relief and deliverance will come to the Jews from another quarter, but you and your family will perish. Who knows? Maybe you have been raised to the throne for a time like this!" 15Then Esther sent this message to Mordecai: 16"Go, gather all the Jews in Susa and fast for me. Don't eat nor drink anything for three days and nights. My maids and I will fast as well. Then I will go in to the king, although it is contrary to the law, and if I die, I die." 17Mordecai did everything Esther had directed.

A Persian law declared that anyone coming to the king in his inner court without a personal invitation, did so under penalty of death. There was no exception - but one. If one dared to come unbidden, and the king happened to be in a gracious mood and held out his scepter in welcome, the death sentence would be set aside.

> (In an aside from our parable – there is a beautiful analogy we can make here to Hebrews 1:8, *"But to the Son He says, 'Your scepter of righteousness is the scepter of Your kingdom..."* Continuing in Hebrews 4:16, we read, *"Let us therefore come boldly to the throne of grace, that we may obtain mercy and find grace to help in time of need."* We have a standing invitation to come into the 'inner court' before God's throne. And when we come, He holds out His scepter to us, not because we happened to come on a day that He was feeling benevolent in mercy - but because of His unchanging righteousness. We need never tremble as we approach, but come boldly, with no fear that we will be refused or

turned away. We have His promise that an extended scepter will always assure us of our welcome into His presence.)

Entering at Her Own Risk

Returning then to our parable, we see that this Persian law of 'enter at your own risk' perfectly symbolizes the fact that we have the same law for ourselves. Ruling our Self-kingdom, we are very quick to 'kill' any thought, or idea, or request, or command that seeks entry to the throne room of our mind. If we do not agree with it, if we do not like it, if it threatens to take us outside our comfort zone, it is quickly squelched. Only if the incoming information in some way interests us, do we 'hold out the scepter' of our 'will' and allow it to enter for our consideration.

I'm Not the One for the Job

When Esther first receives Mordecai's command, she sends back word that it is not possible for her to fulfill his request. How often we, too, argue with God. Moses reminded God that he could not speak, Gideon excused himself because he was 'the least of the least', Sarah laughed in God's face because she was too old, and Jonah thought he could just run away. We think we can inform Him as to what would be right in our situation, or advise Him on why what He is requiring of us will not work. We point out the difficulties to Him as if they had somehow escaped His notice, or He just did not have the insight to understand. How foolish we are when we speak to God as if we know better than He does. Mordecai did not accept Esther's excuses and neither does God accept ours.

No Place to Hide

Mordecai tells Esther that she cannot hide or escape from what is coming upon her people. If nothing is done, she, too, will perish along with everyone else. We do not realize that when we are careless in one area of our life, all other areas are affected as well. We can't refuse to eat and then be surprised that our stomach hurts, our body is weak and we feel light-headed. We can't think grumbling thoughts and expect to feel happy and contented. Nor can we turn a blind eye to one problem because we are afraid that dealing with it will threaten another part of our life that we don't want to change. Everything in our 'kingdom' is related to everything in our 'kingdom', and our choices and decisions have far reaching effects.

Whatsoever You Shall Ask

Esther reconsiders her response to Mordecai's command and, then, humbling herself, submits in obedience to him. She does, however, send back one request of Mordecai. This time, instead of refusing her, he does all that she asks of him.

Can we ever 'command' the Holy Spirit? No, not command, however, we are encouraged to ask with confidence. I John 5:14,15 says, ***"Now this is*** *the confidence that we have in Him, that if we ask anything according to His will, He hears us, and if He hears us, whatever we ask, we know that we have the petitions that we have asked of Him."* When Esther asked Mordecai to take the clothes she sent him as a covering for his grief, he refused her request, but when she asked for something that was according to his will, he willingly consented. And that is when we, too, will find the answers to our prayers - not according to our own will and desires - but when we ask according to what we need in order to do His will.

The Discipline of Denial

We see that Esther asks Mordecai for help in gathering together all the Jews in the kingdom, to ask them to fast for her and with her. This pictures how we often do not have the strength in ourselves to do what we know we must, but the Holy Spirit will always respond to our request for help. Esther takes time to fast, to strengthen herself for the task before her. The discipline of fasting, separating ourselves from the things that distract, in order to spend time alone with God, strengthens the things of God within us. Bringing our flesh under subjection, enables and edifies us. As Paul puts it in I Corinthians 9:27, *"But I discipline my body and bring it into subjection, lest when I have preached to others, I myself should become disqualified."*

We can fast from more things than just food, but fasting from food, disciplines the body in order to bring it in submission to, and in unity with, the Holy Spirit. Then, we go forth in confidence, knowing that His *"grace is sufficient"* for us, and *"His strength is made perfect in weakness."* (II Corinthians 12:9) We can do the work that needs to be done. When the things of the Lord are strong in us, then the things of the flesh shrivel and die.

If I Perish

Esther's words, "If I perish, I perish," are the ultimate expression of submissive obedience to anything the Spirit would call us to do. It reminds us of the song of Habakkuk found in Habakkuk 3:17, 18. *"Though the fig tree may not blossom, nor fruit be on the vines, though the labor of the olive may fail, and the fields yield no food, thought the flock be cut off from the fold, and there be no herd in the stalls, yet I will rejoice in the Lord, I will joy in the God of my salvation."* Or we think of the words of Job, who in the midst of his life's greatest trial, shouted, *"Though He slay me, yet will I trust him!"* -Job 13:15.

Our faith will be tested and tried until it is strong enough to make the Habakkuk and Job and Esther kind of declarations, where obedience to the word of God is more important to us than life itself!

I Peter 1:6-7, *"In this you greatly rejoice, though now for a little while, if need be, you have been grieved by various trials, that the genuineness of your faith, being much more precious than gold that perishes, though it is tested by fire, may be found to praise, honor, and glory at the revelation of Jesus Christ."*

For Such a Time as This

What we go through today, is God preparing us for our tomorrow. We are familiar with the famous words of Mordecai to Esther, *"Who knows but that you were brought to the kingdom for such a time as this."* Do you believe that there could be one moment, one day in your life that might be so important, it will be your defining purpose? We all look for significance, we want our life to matter, to count for something worthwhile. But maybe those days that are so discouraging you want to give up, those days that are so difficult you think you'll never live through them, those days that are so dark that there is no hope in sight, maybe - just maybe - they are the very preparation and equipping you need to bring you to your defining moment! If we look at Esther, we see much cause for sorrow or fear in her life. She lost both parents, leaving her an orphan. She was raised by an uncle, who appears to be unmarried. She is taken by officials of a pagan king to be forced into a harem of women who are used according to the king's desire. Yet, those were all preparations for her 'defining moment' - the act for which Esther is still remembered thousands of years later. Why would you and I be so different? God said that He has a plan and purpose for you, and for me. Let us trust Him to know what is needful in our lives to bring us to where we fulfill that purpose that will have eternal significance. Let us not grow weary and give up! Think of Esther and do not become discouraged.

> *"And let us not grow weary while doing good, for in due season we shall reap if we do not lose heart."* ~Galatians 6:9.

> *"For I know the thoughts that I think toward you, says the Lord, thoughts of peace and not of evil, to give you a future and a hope,"* ~Jeremiah 29:11.

CHAPTER FOURTEEN

Up to Half of the Kingdom

Esther 5:1-3

On the third day, Esther put on her regalia and stood in the inner court of the royal palace opposite the king's house. The king was sitting on his throne in the palace, opposite the entrance. 2When he saw Esther the queen standing in the court, she won his favor, and he held out to her the golden scepter that was in his hand. So Esther approached and touched the top of the scepter. 3Then the king said to her, "What is it, Queen Esther? Whatever your request is, it will be granted, even if it is the half of the kingdom."

We are told the king sits on his throne in the inner court, facing the entrance of his palace. We also sit on the throne of our will, facing anything that comes into 'our inner court'. No thought escapes us, no bit of information slips in unnoticed, but it all passes through our will - subject to what we 'will' to do with it. Our will is the law.

I remember as a child reading fairy tales, and my heart

would always beat faster when a king or ruler would speak these words to some deserving subject, "What do you want? I will give you anything up to half of my kingdom!" Here in our parable, we have the king speaking these words to Esther.

Captain of our Own Ship

We are very accustomed to ruling our own kingdom. We fiercely protect our right to determine our own destiny - be the captain of our own ship. But when we are 'born again', we must begin to shift our 'Self-rule' to yielding our will to be subject to the will of God. Paul, in Romans 12:2, says, ***"and do not be conformed to this world, but be transformed by the renewing of your mind, that you may prove what is that good and acceptable and perfect will of God."*** There is a change in how we perceive and respond to incoming thoughts, or information, and there must be a change in how we understand and relate to God to whom we now belong.

The Scepter of Welcome

We see that Ahasuerus is changing. When Esther takes a deep breath, and steps over the threshold into the throne room where Ahasuerus sits, we expect that everyone in the palace is hovering nearby and holding their breath. Then, when Ahasuerus' eyes turn toward her and his face softens and his scepter is quickly extended in welcome, we can almost hear the collective gasp of relief that whooshes through the throne room. His favor, much as it was hoped for, is unexpected.

As we begin to grow in our walk of faith, we too begin to do the unexpected that is contrary to the worldly thinking we once ruled our life by. We change our thought life, where everything begins. There are changes in how sensitive we are to our spirit; we are hearing and feeling receptive to the messages of the Holy Spirit. In how we perceive and judge and react, we are moving from carnal to spiritual.

Your Wish is My Command – To a Point

Ahasuerus offers up to half his kingdom to Esther. Since Esther represents our spirit and Ahasuerus our will, how do we offer up to half our kingdom? We do not easily step down from our throne, and to offer half of our kingdom is certainly generous. If we are really serious in our new life, and take Romans 12:2 to heart, why not give up the whole of our kingdom? Because to give it all is not possible - half is all we can offer, and still retain control of our own will. While we are to yield to the voice of God, be led by the Holy Spirit, and walk in the spirit instead of the flesh, we never lose our free will, nor are we to give away controlling interest. Our free will comes with the God-given responsibility for our own participation in the sanctifying process. It is only with our willing consent that God will work in and through us. We are admonished in Galatians 5:15, 25, ***"I say then, 'Walk in the Spirit and you shall not fulfill the lust of the flesh…. If we live in*** *the Spirit, we will walk in the Spirit."* If we read all the New Testament verses about obedience like Romans 6:16 which says, *"Do you not know that to whom you present yourselves slaves to obey…. Whether of sin to death, or of obedience to righteousness?"* and other verses like, I Thessalonians 3:14 or I Peter 4:17, we see that, over and over again, we are admonished to 'obey'. Obedience is never something God forces as He could if He controlled one hundred percent of our will. Obedience to God is always by our choice, an act of our 'will'. So in that sense we always stay on the throne, having rule over our own kingdom. The difference is to whom we have given 'the half of our kingdom'.

CHAPTER FIFTEEN

Invitations to a Banquet

Esther 5:4-8

Esther said, "If it seems best to the king, let the king and Haman come today to the banquet that I have prepared for him." 5Then the king said; "Bring Haman quickly, so that Esther's wish may be gratified." So the king and Haman went to the banquet that Esther had prepared. 6While they were drinking wine, the king said to Esther, "Whatever your petition is, it will be granted. Your request, it will be done --- even if it takes half of my kingdom." 7Esther answered, 8"If I have won the king's favor and if it seems best to the king to grant my petition and to accede to my request, my petition and my request are that the king and Haman come to the banquet which I will prepare for them. Tomorrow I will answer the king's question as he wishes."

If you were promised anything you could wish for, what would it be? I don't know what Ahasuerus expected

Esther to ask for, but we are puzzled why Esther does not tell the king immediately what the problem is. He has promised her anything up to half the kingdom. Why not grab the opportunity to speak up and save her people? But no, she ignores his offer and simply invites Ahasuerus to a banquet along with Haman. Obviously, the king was not so clueless as to think his presence at her banquet was her request, because he asks her again, after he has enjoyed the meal she had prepared, what she would desire of him. Esther demurely delays her answer yet again and invites him and Haman to another banquet.

A Rash Promise

We have another biblical account of a king making this rash 'up to half my kingdom' kind of promise. We find the story in Mark 6:14-29. King Herod had been entertained by his wife Herodias' daughter and her dance pleased him. Probably having had too much to drink, he thoughtlessly promised the girl anything she desired, up to half of his kingdom. And he swore to seal his promise. It isn't hard to see that Herod had been set up, because the daughter immediately goes to her mother to ask what she is to do now. And the request was made - John the Baptist's head on a platter. Though the king regretted making the promise, the promise had to be kept and the order was carried out. When we make the offer 'up to half my kingdom', may it not be a rash promise to someone who does not have our best interests at heart, but may it be that we willingly say 'your will, not mine', and submit ourselves to obey the Lord our God, who has only our best in mind.

Delaying for Advantage

Esther does not blurt out her request at first opportunity but uses a delay tactic by extending the banquet invitations. In choosing to wait before presenting her need, she avoids making the mistakes we make when we blindly rush into resolving a problem. So often, we act before we have enough information or understanding to ensure our actions will bring about the desired results.

When the Israelites were about to enter the Promised Land, God said something insightful about the ability of the people to take possession of the land. He said, regarding the enemy in the land, *"I will not drive them out from before you in one year, lest the land become desolate and the beast of the field become too numerous for you,"* ~Exodus 23:29. There is a truth here that reveals how God deals with each believer. He watches over how much we can handle and what we need to learn, and He gives us the time we require to be strong enough to fulfill His will for us. God rarely explains to us the 'whole picture' of where He is taking us or what His plan is. He gives us only enough light to see the next step, which we have to take in faith in spite of the fact that it may not make any sense to us. Second guessing God's plan and rushing ahead will only get us into trouble. Or if we knew the end goal God had in mind, we would immediately run off on our own, trusting in our own wisdom, our own resources, and our own ability to get there. If we only have enough insight for one step, our dependence remains on God.

So giving us what we need, as we need it, is not only our safeguard but it also exercises our faith to trust in Him. It also explains why some new believers will grow in leaps and bounds in one area of their life, but seem to be oblivious to something in another area that others are quick to point out and criticize them for. The sanctification, or maturing process, in our lives is a personal one and takes a life-time. We have to agree with Paul in Philippians 3:12, ***"Not that I have already attained, or am already perfected… but I press on."***

Ahasuerus is not ready to hear Esther's request. He is still too carnal in his understanding and maturity and his motives are still self-focused. Therefore, Esther wisely waits until Ahasuerus, himself, is in a place where granting her request will come from the desire of his will.

Growing in Relationship

I would like to draw another analogy out of Esther's banquet invitations. We have not seen much interaction or fellowship between Ahasuerus and Esther to this point. In fact, Esther hesitated to approach Ahasuerus because she had not been called into his presence for thirty days. Does that not immediately parallel with our tendency to neglect feeding our spirit? Can we go thirty days without thinking about God? Without considering Him, and letting His word guide us in our choices and decisions?

Without edifying our spirit in prayer and thanksgiving and praise? Esther, with her banquet invitations, is wooing Ahasuerus, drawing him in to fellowship with her, that he might experience the difference between spending time with Haman or with her. At this point, we see Ahasuerus is still keeping company with them both - just as the immature believer is still entertaining the flesh, even though he is also learning to listen to his 'new spirit' and the things of God that will bring the needful changes into his life.

Standing Invitation to Dinner

So much could be said about the symbolism involving the banquets. How much of our life is centered on food and eating? Any event that is important to us will involve a banquet, fellowship around the table. Food for life is a God-given need that is pleasurable for us to fulfill. God purposely made food a vital necessity in our lives, so that when He speaks of our need for Him in terms of food, we understand how important it is. As new believers, we are to be as hungry for God's word as a baby is for milk, *"As newborn babes, desire the pure milk of the word that you may grow thereby."* ~I Peter 2:2. Then as we mature, we are to desire more than just milk because, *"Solid food belongs to those who are of full age, that is, those who by reason of use have their senses exercised to discern both good and evil,"* ~ Hebrews 5:14. Jesus also describes His desire for fellowship with us in terms of eating together. In Revelation 3:20, Jesus says, *"Behold, I stand at the door and knock. If anyone hears My voice and opens the door, I will come in to him and dine with him, and he with me."* You and I have a standing invitation to dinner. Do we eagerly accept, as Ahasuerus did, or do we let our Lord stand at the door and knock – waiting? And let us not forget that we have the greatest banquet of all to look forward to - the marriage supper of the Bridegroom and His bride. *"Blessed are those who are called to the marriage supper of the Lamb!"* ~Revelation 19:9.

Esther 5:9-14

Haman went out that day joyful and elated, but when he saw Mordecai in the king's gate and noticed that he neither stood up nor moved for him, he was furiously angry with Mordecai. 10Nevertheless Haman restrained himself and went home. He called together his friends and Zeresh his wife 11and recounted to them the greatness of his wealth, how many children he had, and all the ways in which the king had honored him, and how he had promoted him above the officials and the royal courtiers. 12"What is more," Haman said, "Queen Esther brought no one in with the king to the banquet which she had prepared except me, and tomorrow also I am invited by her along with the king. 13Yet all this does not satisfy me as long as I see Mordecai the Jew sitting at the king's gate." 14Then Zeresh his wife and all his friends said to him, "Let a gallows seventy-five feet high be erected, and in the morning speak to the king and let Mordecai be hanged on it. Then go merrily with the king to the banquet." The advice pleased Haman, and so he had the gallows erected.

We have a new character walk into our parable - Haman's wife, whose name is Zeresh. I found her name meaning interesting - misery, strange, dispersed inheritance. Considering that a wife is a helpmeet to her husband - someone who supports him - we find the meaning of Zeresh to be a fitting description of that which supports our flesh. **'Misery'** is a familiar bedfellow to those who indulge their flesh. **'Strange'** describes the philosophy that supports and encourages the flesh to fulfill its desires - strange because it is totally contrary to the way we were created to be. And **'dispersed inheritance'** is the most revealing. The flesh is always seeking that which will enrich it and ensure its future well-being, but there is no inheritance … it has been dispersed, or disseminated, like feathers in the wind, always just out of reach! The promises of the flesh are empty, there is no inheritance.

Roller Coaster of Emotions

In this section of our parable, we see the pride of Haman exposed in full view. We see him leave the banquet hall extremely joyful with a glad heart, his emotions are on a positive high. He thinks he has it made - life is good! But note how quickly he is knocked down. One glance at Mordecai and he goes from peak-high to pit-low. Isn't that how it is when we live in the flesh? It is a rollercoaster of emotions with no stabilizer to keep us steady. The happiness high we feel when we experience something that we enjoy in the flesh is leaning on circumstance, and is dependent on what is happening at the moment. This is in such stark contrast to the joy we have in the Lord - which is dependent on HIM - and since He never changes, our joy is not conditional on external happenings; it rests in our relationship with Him.

The sight of Mordecai fills Haman with wrath. What did Mordecai do to offend him? He ignored him; he did not stand to salute him or tremble with fear in his presence. There is nothing that offends pride like being ignored, to be made to feel invisible, or insignificant; it demands to be acknowledged and exalted.

And when pride is offended, where does it go but somewhere it can be built up, somewhere it will be soothed and bowed down to. Haman seeks out his wife and his friends who are closest to him. Having a captive audience, he brags about all his accomplishments, enumerating them one by one: his great riches, his multitude of children, his rise to power, and his position of authority in the kingdom. And if that wasn't proof enough of his great honor, he accentuates how he was the only one to be invited by the queen to dine with her and the king. Basking in the heat of Haman's pride, his wife and friends are quick to affirm him in his prominence. But, suddenly, the tide of Haman's emotion turns, and he explodes in a torrent of wrath. Everything - every single thing - on his long list of accolades is worth nothing at all to him as long as that Jew, that Mordecai, sits at the king's gate!

As extreme as Haman's reaction is, it does picture for us our own weakness. Our flesh takes pride in what we possess, everything we have earned, or achieved … but … there is always a 'but'. We could be happy, except for that one thing that is lacking! The flesh is never content with what it has, it is always focused on what it does not have. We read these words in I Timothy 6:8, *"And having food and clothing, with these we shall be content."* Is Paul saying that we should not have anything more than the bare necessities? No, because just a few verses down, he says that God, *"gives us richly all things to enjoy."* The point Paul is making is that if we cannot be content with what we have, having more will not satisfy us. This summer my granddaughter spent a couple of weeks in a village in East Timor, where the living conditions are very primitive - no running water or indoor plumbing, only hanging fabric over the window or door openings in the huts. The people have little more than bare necessities, yet their contentment shines on their happy, smiling faces!

Extreme Measures of Retribution

The advice that appeals to the flesh is always self-serving to the extreme, just as we see pictured in the advice given to Haman by his wife and friends. Their solution to Haman's problem is to, *"Make a gallows, and ask the king to hang Mordecai on it, and then go merrily to the banquet."* We read in, II Peter 2:18, a description of those who give wrong advice, *"…for when they speak great swelling words of emptiness they allure through*

the lust of the flesh…" How ignorant the flesh is of what is to come, how naively it ignores any consequences, or dire repercussions. Only the self-indulgent demands of the moment matter, as we see from Haman's reaction. He is so pleased with the advice, he immediately orders the gallows built. There is something noteworthy in the instructions Haman gives to the builder of the gallows. Gallows high enough to hang a man would need to be no more than ten feet high, even on the generous side, but we see Haman ordering gallows a staggering 75 feet high! I think the obvious analogy here is how outrageous our unforgiving anger, our wounded pride, is in what it demands in retaliation or retribution. Perhaps another reason the gallows are so high is to ensure that all will see the great 'height' of the undeserved humiliation that has been suffered at the hands of the offender. Perhaps, then, we will feel better, but of course we never do.

CHAPTER SIXTEEN

Sleepless in Susa

Esther 6:1-3

On that night the king was unable to sleep, so he gave orders to bring the books that recorded memorable deeds, and they were read before the king. 2It was found recorded how Mordecai had furnished information regarding Bigthan and Teresh, two of the king's attendants who guarded the entrance of the palace, who had attempted to kill King Ahasuerus. 3"What honor and dignity have been conferred on Mordecai for this?" the king asked. When the king's pages who waited on him replied "Nothing has been done for him,"

In the quiet darkness of the night, we think our best thoughts; we think our worst thoughts; we dream sweet dreams; we experience tormenting nightmares; we drift into sweet slumber, or we lie sleepless as we toss and turn, mocked by worry and anxiety.

Reading at Night

The night after the banquet, the king could not sleep. We are not told why he could not sleep. We are not even told if he was troubled; we are only told that sleep did not come to him. So he did what I do when I cannot sleep - read a book. The book he called for was the book preferred by kings because it is the chronicles of the happenings in their kingdom. We have thirty-eight references to the 'book of the chronicles of the kings' referred to the Old Testament. One reference is found in II Kings 23:28, ***"Now the rest of the acts of Josiah, and all that he did, are they not written in the book of the chronicles of the kings of Judah?"***

Do you see the phrase, "and all that he did"? What do we do if we lay awake at night but go over 'the record of the chronicles' of all that we have done? Our memory has recorded it all in great detail and is willing to turn the pages for us as long as we stay awake.

Belated Gratitude

As Ahasuerus reads during that sleepless night, he comes across a record of palace intrigue he had forgotten about. He is reminded of his doorkeepers' conspiracy against him and how narrowly he escaped with his life. Now, he learns that it was Mordecai who uncovered the sinister plot and sent the warning that saved him. Feeling a sense of gratitude, and a desire to honor Mordecai for his good deed, he asks what has been done for Mordecai and the answer is given, "Nothing."

Sometimes as a new believer, we do not immediately experience a profound sense of gratitude for what the Lord has done for us. As we grow in our knowledge and understanding of who the Lord is and see the evidence of His goodness toward us, our emotions respond with thanksgiving. Our heart overflows with a desire to praise Him and to honor Him in our kingdom.

CHAPTER SEVENTEEN

Whom the King Honors
is Honored Indeed

Esther 6:4-10

The king said, "Who is in the court?" Now Haman had just entered the outer court of the king's house to speak to the king about hanging Mordecai on the gallows that he had prepared for him. 5So the king's pages said to him, "Haman is standing there; in the court." The king said, "Let him enter." 6So Haman entered, and the king said to him, "What should be done for the man whom the king wishes to honor?" Haman said to himself, "Whom besides me could the king wish to honor?" 7So Haman said to the king, "For the man whom the king wishes to honor 8let a royal garment be brought, which the king has worn, and the horse on which the king has ridden and on whose head a royal diadem has been placed. 9Then let the garment and the horse be placed in charge of one of the king's noble officials. Let him clothe the man whom the king wishes to honor and let him lead that man on the horse through the city square, proclaiming before him, 'This is what is done for the man whom the king wishes to honor.'" 10Then the king said to Haman, "Make haste and take the garment and the horse, as you have said, and do this to Mordecai the Jew, who sits in the king's gate. Omit nothing of all you have said."

Seemingly unrelated details that come together in a way that catches our attention is called a coincidence. We speak of coincidences as occurring by random chance, yet Oswald Chambers rightly recognized 'coincidences' as an indication that God is at work. He so aptly said, "God is the God of the haphazard", by haphazard meaning coincidences. Where there is a coincidence in your life - look for God, He is nearby. There are several coincidences in this part of our parable. Ahasuerus 'happens' to not be able to sleep; he 'happens' to read about Mordecai's unrewarded good deed. Ahasuerus could not wait to remedy this oversight and gets up so early he doesn't seem to expect anyone to be in the court, but when he asks who is there, it 'happens' to be Haman. Haman just 'happened' to be filled with wrath at Mordecai the day before. He also probably 'happened' to have a sleepless night, and he goes to make his appeal to the king as early as possible. It just 'happens' that on the very day Haman seeks Mordecai's death, the king seeks his honor. All these details could only come together if someone was working them together for a specific purpose. We know that God works together for our good; the seemingly random things in our life are never random in the hands of God, as we read in Romans 8:28, *"And we know that all things word together for good to those who love God, to those who are the called according to His purpose."*

Our sense of justice rejoices to see that, finally, Ahasuerus is going to reward Mordecai for his good deed that has gone unacknowledged, but, then, we are staggered by the fact that he would consult Haman on how best to honor him. Really?? But stop to think - something happens that requires some action or decision on our part. We think … "Hmmm … I wonder what I could do?" Our mind is open for suggestions, and most often it is the voice of our carnal nature that we hear first. When we want advice on how to work something to our advantage; when we crave some creature comfort; when we are planning a day off or a vacation - is it not our 'flesh' that we consult first? We trust our flesh to know what will make us feel good. As Ephesians 5:29 says, *"For no one ever hated his own flesh, but nourishes and cherishes it …."* And did Jesus not, Himself, advise us to consult our own flesh when we want to know how to love or honor someone else? *"….you shall love your neighbor as yourself…"* ~Mark 12:31.

That's NOT What I Meant

So, of course, we see Haman give excellent advice on how to honor someone the king wants to honor. We also see how his own self-serving plans were totally derailed. Haman - as powerful as he is, as conniving and vengeful his intent - cannot do anything without Ahasuerus' approval. We live in a victim mentality society, but we can only take on that cloak if we 'will it'. How many life stories have inspired us and captivated our attention, people who rose above their horrendous circumstances and lived a life admired by all! I think of Nick Vujicic, born without arms and legs, who is an example of someone who used his disability to such an advantage it became his ability, and he is a sought after motivational speaker who has given hope and encouragement to thousands of people. Our 'will', the throne upon which we rule, has the power and authority to order our 'kingdom' in such a way that we need never cower in a victim mentality or allow circumstance to overrule the good God has ordained for us. We exercise our free will to work for our good, or we allow it to work against us.

Note the things Haman desires for himself - the cloak the king wore, the King's own horse marked by the royal crest, and 'celebrity status' as in basking in the adulation of the crowds. No point in being honored in private. He desires everything that symbolizes the role of the king. Wearing his clothes gives him the façade of appearance, like the king. Riding his horse gives him the sense of power to conquer and to command, like the king. And the crowds adoring him feed his ego - in his mind, he elevates himself to be equal to the king. Note that he stops short of asking for the crown. Had the king given Haman his crown, he would have effectively abdicated his throne and given his ruling power to another. Haman in asking for what he did, stopped short of requesting the throne itself.

How aware are we of our flesh in its desire to be honored? Do we, at times, give our 'cloak' or our 'horse' to our flesh and allow the roles to be reversed - instead of the 'will' ruling the flesh, our flesh rules our will? When we experience an insult, or affront, or hurt, do we immediately abdicate the throne in favor of the flesh and allow it to dictate the revenge that is our perceived right? Or, do we use the wisdom of Ahasuerus and consult the flesh only in order to know how to best honor the One that deserves to be honored?

Esther 6:11-14

So Haman took the garment and the horse and clothed Mordecai, and made him ride through the city square and proclaimed before him, "This is what is done for the man whom the king wishes to honor." 12Mordecai returned to the king's gate, but Haman hurried to his house, mourning, with his head covered. 13Haman recounted to Zeresh his wife and to all his friends everything that had happened to him. Then his wise men and Zeresh his wife said to him, "If Mordecai before whom you have already been humiliated is of the Jewish people, you can do nothing against him but will surely fall before him." 14While they were still talking with him, the king's attendants came and quickly took Haman to the banquet that Esther had prepared.

Mordecai receives the praise and worship offered him, but he does nothing more than receive it. After he has been honored, he returns to his place at the gate of the king's palace. He could take advantage of the honor heaped upon him and act on some initiative to take a more visible position of authority in the kingdom. But he doesn't, which is the very opposite from what we know Haman would do. In this Mordecai pictures the Holy Spirit in our lives - ever the gentleman, never one to force his will over ours, filling only the places in our life that we offer to him. It is only as we willingly submit our will to His that He exercises authority in our lives. In contrast, our carnal flesh, looks for and grabs any opportunity to overrule our will and insist on its own way with no consideration for consequences that could destroy our well-being - both in this life and the one to come.

We see another insightful truth, here, praising, and worshiping God, humiliates the flesh. If we feel weak or if we feel tempted, let us follow Ahasuerus' example and 'parade' God in the streets of our kingdom. In our thoughts, our words, our actions, remembering what He has done for us - being thankful and full of praise for all His goodness. And like Haman, our flesh will hang its head. If we humble our flesh, God Himself will honor us. ***"Humble yourselves in the sight of the Lord, and He will lift you up,"*** -James 4:10.

Have you ever noticed that the flesh is a fair weather friend? As soon as something goes wrong, the flesh abandons you to your misery and demise. So we see Haman, coming home from his humiliating experience, hoping perhaps for a little comfort from his wife and friends, but all he receives is cold cynicism, echoing his worst fears. He has begun to fall and will continue to fall. There is no hope for him - except for one last glimmer - he still has another dinner invitation.

CHAPTER EIGHTEEN

Revelation Time

Esther 7:1-4

So the king and Haman went to drink with Queen Esther. 2As they were drinking wine on that second day, the king again said to Esther, "Whatever your petition is, Queen Esther, it will be granted to you. Whatever you request it will be done, even if it takes half of the kingdom." 3Then Queen Esther answered, "Your Majesty, if I have won your favor, and if it seems best to Your Majesty, let my life be given me as my petition, and my people as my request, 4for I and my people have been sold to be destroyed, killed, and completely annihilated! If we had been merely sold into slavery I would not have disturbed your peace, because such a fate would not have affected the interests of the king."

Esther's invitation to dinner was not an invite to a two hour affair as we expect a dinner invitation to be. This banquet went on for days. It is at the end of the second day, of this second banquet, that the king repeats his question to Esther - what it is that she desires, up to half his kingdom. And this time, Esther finally tells him. She has not only gained confidence by dining with Ahasuerus, (intimate fellowship) but has also built up in him a receptive frame of mind. Even on a carnal level, are we not more attune to something we have been made to be curious about for some time?

An Odd Comment

There is an odd comment that Esther makes in her request. She says that if, instead of being sold to be killed or annihilated, they had only been sold to be slaves - male and female - she would not have said anything. To understand this comment and be able to glean some insight into what this comment could mean for us, we need to find supporting scripture for some background understanding.

An enlightening passage is found in Deuteronomy 28:68. The setting for this verse is in context of the whole passage, from verse 58 on, where God is warning the Israelites about what would happen to them if they did not carefully obey the law, being guilty of *"no longer fearing the Lord their God".* He warns that, as a result of their continued disobedience, they would be scattered among the nations and find no rest. At that time, the Lord would take them back to bondage in Egypt. We find these words in verse 68, *"And the Lord will take you back to Egypt in ships, by the way of which I said to you, You shall never see it again. And there you shall be offered for sale to your enemies as male and female slaves, but no one will buy you.* "We might be tempted, at first, to think, "Ohh ... God is saying they would be offered as slaves but no one would buy them ... so that is good! They wouldn't be owned by anyone and, therefore, they would be spared." But the Hebrew word for 'buy' carries the meaning we understand from the word 'redeem'. God is warning that, because of their sin and rebelliousness, the punishment would be that they would return to where God never intended them to be - back to the slavery He had saved them from. This time, there would be no one to redeem them or set them free. We see in this passage that being sold as slaves was the result of continued disobedience and was a deserved punishment for their sin.

Listening to Esther's remark with this contextual understanding in mind, we understand what she was saying. The implication is that, if she and her people had been sold into slavery as a result of wrongdoing, then she would have taken her deserved punishment without protest. We have a New Testament verse admonishing us to do the same, to patiently accept our punishment for wrongdoing and not protest against it - nor expect any praise! In I Peter 2:20, we read, *"For what credit is it if, when you are beaten for your faults, you take it patiently?"*

Esther and her people, however, are not guilty, nor have they been sold into slavery, but they have been condemned by an enemy to death, complete annihilation; therefore, she cannot keep silent.

"Sold into Slavery"

Esther's 'odd comment' is easily overlooked as we read the parable, but I think there are things we can learn by considering it.

We naturally gravitate to extremes - perhaps because they are so clearly defined. It is easier to proclaim God as a God of unconditional love or a God of wrath ready to condemn sinners than it is to discern the true character of God that demands an understanding of both His love and His holiness. God desires a holy people, separated from sin, 'slaves' of righteousness.

God IS love, a God who desires that all men be saved. Two things, however, must also be considered; God has given man free will and God cannot allow sin into His Presence. But the choice has to be ours, ***"Do you not know that to whom you present yourselves slaves to obey, you are that one's slaves whom you obey, whether of sin to death, or of obedience to righteousness?"*** ~Romans 6:16. There are times when God, as a loving parent, withdraws His hand and allows us to go our own stubborn way so we experience the painful results of beings 'slaves' to the flesh. But God only withdraws His hand, allowing us to be 'sold as slaves', out of a desire to bring us back into obedience and joyful fellowship with Him.

So being brought under chastisement - 'sold into slavery'- can be for our good as we read in I Peter 4:1-2, ***"....he who has suffered in the flesh has ceased from sin, that he no longer should live ... in the flesh ... but for the will of God."*** We know how Paul, to keep him from pride, was given a thorn in his flesh that caused him to suffer - but its purpose was to keep him from sin. Through it Paul learned to lean on God's grace and experience that it was sufficient, even in weakness.

We are also warned about wandering too far away from God - where we will be consumed by our sinful desires and suffer eternal death. We read in James 1:15 says, *"Then when desire has conceived, it gives birth to sin and sin when it is full-grown, brings forth death."* And, in Hebrews 6:4-6, we see that there is a falling away into sin so deep that we lose our desire to repent and return. *"For it is impossible ... if they fall away, to renew them again to repentance, since they crucify again for themselves the Son of God and put Him to an open shame."*

Even though we are in a new covenant relationship with God - one built on forgiveness - we need to walk in obedience, heeding the warnings God has always given His people. And His heart cry is the same today as it was so long ago when His words were spoken by his prophet in Ezekiel 33:11, *"Say to them, 'As I live,' says the Lord God, 'I have no pleasure in the death of the wicked, but that the wicked turn from his way and live. Turn, turn, from your evil ways! For why should you die, O House of Israel?'"* There is a place of safety where we need never fear ... *"Keep yourselves in the love of God..."* -Jude 20. Note the word 'keep'. It is in the imperative, something we must choose to do.

Therefore, we see Esther's 'odd comment' to Ahasuerus being symbolic of God working through our spirit to call us back to Him, to repent and turn away from a friendship with the flesh. God will do whatever He can to make it hard for us to go our own way as He says in Acts 9:5 that it is *"hard for you to kick against the goads."*

Can we say with Esther that we will take our punishment / correction / discipline / chastisement without complaint, recognizing that it is administered by the loving hand of God, knowing that it is purposed to draw us back into a holy relationship with Him?

No Compensation for Serving the Flesh

Esther also informs the king that, *"The enemy could never compensate for the king's loss"*. To walk in the flesh, bringing ourselves into bondage to the flesh - no matter how much the flesh promises us in gains - it can never *"compensate for"* what we lose because we did not choose God's way. Going our own way, allowing the flesh to rule, can never bring satisfaction, can never fulfill, can never bring peace or joy to our life. It robs us of all the Lord's blessings in and through us and breaks His sweet fellowship with us.

So, how will Ahasuerus respond to Esther's plea? Let's read on in our parable....

Esther 7:5-6

"Then King Ahasuerus answered and said to Queen Esther, 'Who is he, and where is he, who would dare presume in his heart to do such a thing?' And Esther

said, 'The adversary and enemy is this wicked Haman!'
So Haman was terrified before the king and queen."

The king is on the brink of an 'ah-ha' moment where the light of his understanding goes on. He has not, until this moment, suspected Haman of being anything other than his friend. He had no idea that anyone in his kingdom hated Esther and her people to the point that they wished them dead.

The Company We Keep

Are we not guilty of the same ignorance? How often do we blissfully entertain certain habits or beliefs or modes of entertainment, or character traits, and never have any idea that they are harmful to our spiritual well-being - until the moment a sermon, a book, a comment, a revelation of some kind, opens our eyes and changes our view of things. At first we are shocked, then convicted and, perhaps, even angry. We must, then, make a choice. Are we going to take the first steps toward change in our life, or are we going to resist, being reluctant to make the necessary effort to let go of something we have carnally enjoyed?

CHAPTER NINETEEN

Conflicting Emotions – Fear and Wrath

Esther 7:7-10

In his wrath the king rose from the place where he was drinking wine and went into the palace garden. Haman stayed to beg Queen Esther for his life, for he saw that the king was fully determined to bring calamity upon him. 8As the king returned from the palace garden to the banquet hall, Haman had flung himself on Esther's couch. The king cried, "Is he going to rape my queen while I am present in my own house?" As the king spoke these words, the attendants covered Haman's face 9and Harbonah, one of those who waited on the king, said, "There are the gallows, seventy-five feet high, which Hanan erected for Mordecai, who spoke a good word in behalf of the king, standing in the house of Haman!" The king said "Hang him on them." 10So they hanged Haman on the gallows that he had prepared for Mordecai. Then the wrath of the king was pacified.

We identify with Ahasuerus' wrath against someone who would threaten the life of his queen. We feel the betrayal that adds to the depth of his anger. Discovering that his trusted friend - the one he had elevated to second in the kingdom - is the one who plotted against him, is hard to take. Feeling blindsided, it drives Ahasuerus to seek some space, somewhere he can think and wrap his head around what he has just learned.

A Minor Character

We might almost miss him, but we have a new character, who briefly appears on the stage, named Harbonah. While he seems to be supportive of the king, his name meaning might suggest he is a turn-coat. His Persian name means 'donkey-driver'. Not a very flattering name. A donkey is notoriously stubborn and oft contrary. Maybe an apt description for someone who turns whichever way, at the time, is more advantageous to him. Jewish tradition has it that Harbonah was originally one of Haman's supporters or friends, but when he saw that Haman was in trouble, he quickly jumped ship and went to stand with Ahasuerus. To prove his new loyalty, and maybe also to protect himself from Haman's wrath for betraying him, he is quick to point out the gallows that stand ready in Haman's backyard.

I hope we are not like Harbonah and do not need to learn from him. Do we keep one eye on the wind to see which way it will blow in our favor? Do we follow the things of the Lord when it feels good, then follow the things of the flesh when that feels good? Do we, like those ancient Israelites, too often halt between two opinions? May we not be guilty of having a 'turn-coat' allegiance – unless we are taking a carnal weakness and turning it into a strength for the glory of God's kingdom. Stubbornness is usually looked upon as a negative character trait, unless we are stubborn in our stand for the things of God, it is then a source of strength!

A Personal Hanging

Through the years up to our own present time, Haman being hanged on the gallows he built for someone else, has been applauded and held up as the standard for justice being served.

Do we, however, recognize the spiritual significance on a personal level? We, as believers, are familiar with the command to 'hang' or crucify the flesh … but while we give ready lip service to subduing the flesh, do we actually 'put it to death'? We read in Galatians 5:24, *"And those who are Christ's have crucified the flesh with its passions and desires."* Where is your 'Haman'? Is he still keeping company with your will or have you condemned him to death? Romans 8:13, confirms that the fears of Esther, regarding Haman, are true in our own spiritual battle with the flesh. We read, *"For if you live according to the flesh, you will die but if by the Spirit you put to death the deeds of the body, you will live."* If we allow the flesh free reign - if we allow it to be second in our kingdom - we will die spiritually.

No Communication

It is worthy to note that Esther never speaks to Haman. Even when Haman throws himself upon her, we do not hear a word of protest from her. Again, it is only Ahasuerus who has the authority to deal with Haman. If he does nothing, Haman will have his way and will choke the life out of Ahasuerus' queen, effectively annihilating any resistance to his plans.

So it is in our spiritual life as well. If we do not 'will' against the flesh, it will crush the life out of our spirit leaving us vulnerable and open to all the lies and deception purposed against us. We leave the doors of our flesh open to the incoming influences that will work death in us. Study this truth that Paul expounds for us in II Corinthians 10:3-6, *"For though we walk in the flesh, we do not war according to the flesh. For the weapons of our warfare are not carnal but mighty in God for pulling down strongholds, casting down arguments and every high thing that exalts itself against the knowledge of God, bringing every thought into captivity to the obedience of Christ and being ready to punish all disobedience when your obedience is fulfilled."*

What an amazing passage that is when we hold it up against our parable. Ahasuerus representing our will, is where the battle is won or lost. We walk in the flesh - in a physical body - but it is not with physical weapons that our battles are fought. They are fought in our own mind, our 'will' taking our thoughts and bringing them into line with God's word, leaving no entrance for the enemy to work through the weaknesses of our flesh. Look at the words used to describe our 'will': mighty, pulling down strongholds, casting down anything contrary to the knowledge of God, taking captive! We are not weak; God has given us a throne from which we have the power and authority to rule. But the question is, ARE we ruling? Or have we abdicated and given our authority to the flesh? If we have, we are living in a state of chaos that will leave us too weak to attain to the goal of being the conqueror and overcomer that we are called to be in our kingdom.

If we look at the pieces of the armor of God listed in Ephesians 6:11-17 – shoes, helmet, breastplate, shield, belt, sword - we notice the one offensive weapon is the sword. A sword is a deadly weapon and its only use is to kill the enemy. Our sword is the word of God. How sharp is our sword? Do we have it at the ready, like Jesus did when He was tempted, to defend ourselves effectively against anything that comes against us? The truth of God's word is, and always will be, the only weapon we need to 'kill' any argument or temptation the flesh could bring against us.

Righteous Anger

Emotions of our flesh are like untrained children. The strongest parent quakes before the temper tantrum of their out of control two year old. If the child is not taken in hand and trained, the parent becomes the servant of the child and chaos in the home results. So also our emotions stirred up by some offense against our flesh are loud and demanding. We are pulled into them and our tendency is to do whatever they demand to calm them down. On the other hand, good emotions that follow the right decisions of the will, are the 'felt' reward of having followed righteousness and godly responses. We see a contrast of emotional responses when we look at Esther, Haman, and Ahasuerus in the banquet hall after Esther reveals who Haman is. Esther is calm and controlled, Haman is out of control, and Ahasuerus is furious

Though Ahasuerus responds in anger, we see that he is growing in wisdom by how he deals with his anger. He is now aware of the evil lurking behind the façade presented by his supposed friend Haman and is filled with wrath, but he does the right thing. This time he does not call for his 'wise men'. His anger is a righteous anger, and he reacts appropriately. ***"Be angry and sin not.'*** ~Ephesians 4:26. He removes himself from Haman, and takes the time to consider what he should do. And when he comes back to Esther and Haman, we see immediately what his decision is. He chooses Esther and commands Haman to be killed, never again to have power over him. We can learn from Ahasuerus' example here. How often could we have avoided making emotion-driven decisions and circumvented stressful situations, if we had just taken the time to seek a quiet spot to reflect and pray for wisdom to ascertain what our God-honoring response should be?

Is Our Fear Misplaced?

Our parable uncovers Haman's terror when he sees that he has been exposed. Knowing he is now seen for who he is, he fears for his life. I don't think there is one of us that has not experienced fear when we consider going contrary to our 'flesh'. Doing something that might in some way compromise our security or comfort causes us to 'fear'. If I, like the rich young ruler, am asked to sell all that I have and follow the Lord, how will I support my family? If I speak up at work against that unethical practice, will I make enemies? If I don't do what everyone else thinks is okay to do, what will people think of me? If the stock market crashes tomorrow, what will happen to my nicely ordered, financially secure life? We have a self-protecting instinct that is God-given, but often that instinct is so tied to our flesh that it protects that which, in truth, is our enemy.

CHAPTER TWENTY

A House in Order

Esther 8:1, 2

At that time King Ahasuerus gave the property of Haman the Jews' enemy to Queen Esther. Mordecai was made one of the king's personal advisers, for Esther had disclosed his relationship to her. 2The king also drew off his signet ring, which he had taken from Haman. He gave it to Mordecai, and Esther placed Mordecai in charge of Haman's property.

Our first reaction, in reading the above parable passage, is to ask who would want Haman's house. Burn it down! But this concept of the people of God claiming and inhabiting the land of the wicked is not new. We need only to look back to Israel, to the time when they were finally ready to enter the Promised Land. The Promised Land was not vacant, virgin land; it was inhabited by people who had rejected the God of the Jews. They were worshipping their pagan gods and indulged in their own evil ways.

The pagan inhabitants of the land are a good picture of our flesh. When we become believers, we still inhabit the same 'land' or 'kingdom', but we need to remove everything that hinders who we are as a new creature in Christ. Old habits and ways, however, die hard, and we do not change overnight. God pictures this process for us in how He dealt with His people moving into the Promised Land. In Exodus 23:24, He commands them regarding the inhabitants of the land, ***"You shall not bow down to their gods, nor serve them, nor do according to their works; but you shall utterly overthrow them and completely break down their sacred pillars."*** But then a few verses down He adds, ***"I will not drive them out from before you in one year, lest the land become desolate and the beasts of the field become too numerous for you. Little by little I will drive them out from before you, until you have increased, and you inherit the land."*** In other words, God was guarding them in the Promised Land, never requiring more of them than they were able to do, watching over them as they grew in strength and little by little took control of the land they seized from their 'enemies'. In the same way, God watches over us as well, whether we are a babe in Christ, or whether we are still grasping at the foundational things, are not yet ready for 'meat' or are 'young men' – whatever growth stage we are in, until we are mature, God will work with us and help us as 'little by little' to replace the things of the flesh and give 'the land' to the new godly things of the spirit.

In Close Fellowship

Something very remarkable is happening in our story, something so important we need to take it to heart and not forget it! Up to this point, we have seen Mordecai limited to the peripheral shadows of our parable. We have seen him sitting at the gate, we have seen him pass information to Esther, but we have seen no direct communication between Mordecai and Ahasuerus. Now, finally, we see that Mordecai is center stage - up close with Esther and Ahasuerus. What changed? Haman has been put to death! Until we crucify the flesh, the Holy Spirit stays at the gate, so to speak. We can only expect close fellowship when we are willing to be completely sold out to God.

Perhaps this pictures what Paul was speaking about in Galatians 4:19, where he says, *"My little children, for whom I labor in birth again until Christ is formed in you."* Or in Galatians 3:3, where we read his words, *"Are you so foolish? Having begun in the Spirit, are you now being made perfect by the flesh?"* It is only as we grow in maturity that we begin to recognize the difference between the things of the flesh and the things of the Spirit. The more we are aware of the Holy Spirit in our life, the more we will desire His fellowship, and the deeper our fellowship is, the more victorious our walk of faith will be.

We also see Ahasuerus giving to Mordecai the signet ring that he had taken back from Haman. His loyalty has shifted from Haman to Mordecai … his trust has shifted … his go-to-for- advice source has shifted … the company he keeps has changed. Ahasuerus has radically changed – from the inside out! What a clear picture of our own spiritual crossroad, when we too come to the place where we resolve to serve with steadfast faithfulness our new Lord. We must change who we trust, who we go to for direction and guidance. No longer do we so readily consult the flesh; its voice has been muted. The Spirit of God resides within, and there is a change in our will. We now 'will' to guard a close fellowship with the Spirit of God and keep our spirit sensitive to hear His voice.

There is a chain of command we need to note in this verse. King Ahasuerus gave Haman's house to Esther, but Esther appointed Mordecai to rule over the house. Our spirit is our connection to God … but the Holy Spirit of God is the one we listen to and are guided by.

CHAPTER TWENTY-ONE

Haman is Dead but the Decree Stands

Esther 8:3- 8

Then Esther sought another audience with the king and fell at his feet and with tears begged him to avert the evil planned by Haman the Agagite and to frustrate his designs against the Jews. 4The king held out to her the golden sceptre, and she arose and stood before him. 5And she said, "If it seems best to the king, and if I have won his favor and he thinks it right, and if I please him, let written orders be given to revoke the dispatches devised by Haman son of Hammedatha the Agagite, which he wrote ordering the destruction of the Jews who are in all the king's provinces. 6For how can I bear to look upon the evil that will come to my people? How can I bear to see their destruction?" 7Then King Ahasuerus said to Queen Esther and to Mordecai the Jew, "See, I have given Esther the property of Haman, and they have hanged him on the gallows, because he laid hands upon the Jews. 8Now you write on behalf of the Jews, as seems best to you, in the king's name and seal it with the king's signet ring. For a document that is written in the king's name and sealed with the king's signet ring cannot be revoked."

Haman is dead, but we see Esther in great distress, entreating Ahasuerus with tears, for the 'life' of her people. Why? What could this be picturing for us?

We know we live in a fallen world, where sin and sinners abound. We suffer, if not directly as a result of our own sin, then because of someone else's sin. Even after we recognize where the fault is, even when we acknowledge our own transgressions and we turn away from our sinful flesh, our despair is deep because we still carry the guilt and remorse and the consequences that do not go away. The mess our sin, or someone else's, created is still there. The hurt, the damage remains; we all carry the baggage of our past. And, somehow, we have to deal with it

The Real Problem

In our parable, we see the real problem. If you remember, earlier we stated that Persian law was such that once a decree was written, it could never be changed or overturned. Now, in response to Esther's tearful pleading, we hear Ahasuerus' regretful response. He reiterates that a document written in the king's name and sealed with the king's signet ring cannot be revoked. What is the significance of this parable detail that something once decreed cannot be made null and void? We touched on it earlier, how once we set a thought in motion, it triggers the chain of chemical reactions in our body that determine how we feel and ultimately act. Once a thought is 'thinked', it can never be unthought, unspoken, or undone. Our 'kingdom' law is the same as the Persian law, a decree once written into our memory and stamped by our 'will' can never be repealed or undone.

Is there no solution then? No answer or remedy? Yes, there is one thing that can be done, and thankfully we see it revealed in our parable.

A New Decree Solves the Problem

While Ahasuerus fully understands the Persian law, he ingeniously finds a way around it. He gives Esther and Mordecai the authority to *"write new decrees"*. A new decree cannot overturn a decree already written, but it CAN trump it by overruling it.

We can look at this aspect of the Persian law, and use it to understand how the same law works in our own lives. When we sin, when we willfully miss the mark, rarely is the mess we create simply wiped out when we repent. God forgives, but the consequences often remain. God has the answer. If we are willing to submit to whatever 'new decree' He will write, there is still hope that we will survive and prosper. I Peter 2:20 explains that it is only right to patiently endure the painful consequences of our own sinful choices or actions. *"For what credit is it when you are beaten for your faults, you take it patiently?"* In other words, accepting what we deserve. BUT we also have an encouraging word in Romans 8:28

that says, ***"And we know that all things work together for good to those who love God, to those who are the called according to His purpose."***

There would be no need for God to point out that good things work together for good, we already know that, in fact, we take it for granted! So this verse must be an encouragement for us to know that God can take the difficult things in our life - our messes, our trouble, our broken pieces, our pain and suffering - and when we put them into His hand, He can write new decrees and bring something good into our lives. This is the ultimate evidence of His creative ways. We see after David's sin with Bathsheba that Solomon was born to them; the only baby mentioned in the Bible that has this said about him, ***"...and God loved him."*** ~ II Samuel 12:24.

Submitting to a Higher Authority

Note in the parable, that although Ahasuerus wrote the first decree that caused all the trouble, he has no idea how to deal with the situation he himself created. Instead of trying to come up with his own solution, Ahasuerus defers to Esther and Mordecai to do what seems best to them and write the new decrees as they see fit. How wise of Ahasuerus to not even attempt to find his own solution. Are we wise enough to surrender ourselves under God's wise ways, submitting to His word and will? Or do we prefer to keep some controlling interest in how our life is played out.

For God to take the consequences of our actions and do His creative work with them, we must be willing to let go of our own control over them. As Ahasuerus yielded fully to Esther and Mordecai, so we too must say, "Lord, take my mess, and do with it whatever you will, according to your good purposes." And, of course, He will!

CHAPTER TWENTY-TWO

Overruled

Esther 8:9-14

On the twenty-third day of the third month (that is the month of Sivan), the king's secretaries were summoned and as Mordecai instructed an edict was issued to the Jews, to the satraps and provincial governors and the rulers of each of the one hundred twenty-seven provinces from India to Ethiopia in their own script and their own language, and to the Jews in their own script and language. 10Mordecai wrote in the name of King Ahasuerus. He sealed it with the king's signet ring. Dispatches were sent by mounted couriers who rode the swift, noble steeds, bred of the royal studs. 11In this way the king permitted the Jews who were in every city to gather together and make a stand for their life, to destroy, to kill, and annihilate all the armed forces of any people or province that might be hostile to them, including their children and women, and to take their goods as plunder 12throughout all the provinces of King Ahasuerus on that thirteenth day of the twelfth month (which is called Adar). 13A copy of the edict was to be published as a decree in every province --- publically displayed so that the Jews might be ready for that day and avenge themselves. 14So the couriers who rode the swift, noble steeds went out, hastened and impelled by the king's commands!

The way of escape has been found. A Persian decree could not be overturned, but it could be overruled by a higher decree.

What a beautiful picture this is of our own sinful condition. We stood judged and condemned. The decree of death was against us - we had no way of escape; our own righteousness was worthless. But God, in His mercy, put into place a higher decree. The 'trump' of the new decree was that the death of a perfect, sinless person would supersede the death penalty against us. We now have forgiveness through Jesus' sacrifice and His own perfect righteousness to cover us. Death no longer has any power over us as Jesus proclaim, *"Most assuredly, I say to you, he who hears My word and believes in Him who sent Me has everlasting life, and shall not come into judgment, but has passed from death into life!"* ~John 5:24. And, again, the cross trumped the old decree that was against us, *"having wiped out the handwriting of requirements that was against us, which was contrary to us. And He has taken it out of the way, having nailed it to the cross,* ~Colossians 2:14.

Can Ethnic Cleansing Be a Good Thing?

The term 'ethnic cleansing' has become familiar in our own historical times, and we are rightly horrified at the brutality of the senseless, sweeping slaughter of precious life. We know that Haman called for the extermination of all Jews, but now we see that Mordecai, in his new decree, is calling for a massacre of his own.

The two decrees in our parable look like a tit-for-tat killing, until we look at the symbolic meaning of our parable. When we give control of our life to the guidance of the Holy Spirit … does God not desire for us to do an 'ethnic cleansing' to remove from our thoughts and attitudes and beliefs all that is contrary to Him? God wants everything to be new in us - all ungodly things are to be purged and burned. II Corinthians 5:17, 18 says it perfectly, ***"Therefore, if anyone is in Christ, he is a new creation, old things have passed away, behold, all things have become new. Now, all things are of God, who has reconciled us to Himself …."*** This purging in our parable came only after Ahasuerus was ready to give up control of his kingdom. We see the key words in our above scripture, namely, ***"in Christ"*** and ***"reconciled … to Himself"***, that note what needs to be in place before ***"all things can be made new"***. Everything ***"old"*** must be annihilated, until ***"all things are of God"***. Have we looked into our parable mirror lately, to see if all things are of God in us? Or do we need some more 'ethnic cleansing' to remove some things that are still related to the enemy.

No Mercy

We may object to the violence of the ethnic cleansing in the parable until we think about how sin destroys - even a little sin, as Solomon in his wisdom noted, ***"Catch us the foxes, the little foxes that spoil the vines, for our vines have tender grapes."*** ~Song of Solomon 2:15. We see in the Old Testament, how before the Feast of Passover, God commanded that the Israelites totally cleanse their homes of all leaven. In I Corinthians 5:6-7, we are given the code-word for the Old Testament leaven, indicating that it symbolizes sin. The commandment of God leaves no doubt about the severity of punishment for anyone found with leaven in their home. We read in Ex. 12:15, ***"Seven days you shall eat unleavened bread. On the first day you shall remove leaven from your houses. For whoever eats leavened bread from the first day until the seventh day, that person shall be cut off from Israel."*** This meticulous searching for, and eliminating, all leaven is still observed today in an orthodox Jewish home. The importance of this ritual is burned deep into the Jewish mind, but how diligent are we to have the same attitude in ridding our kingdom of what the leaven symbolizes - the sins of our flesh? The battle isn't over until ***"all things are of God."*** For most of us, that's a lifetime battle that is never completely won, but we keep on fighting. We hear Paul as he speaks to his own battle, ***"But I discipline my body and bring it into subjection, lest when I have preached to others, I myself should become disqualified,"*** ~I Corinthians 9:27.

In the Nick of Time

We are surprised to see that Mordecai's decree is set to be carried out on the very same day that Haman had chosen for the massacre of the Jews. In the nick of time, just as the decree to kill the Jews takes effect, all those who stand in readiness to obey Haman's decree are themselves destroyed. Haman's decree now has no power to harm, since there is no one left to carry it out. Without changing the decree, it is now ineffective to do what was written therein. Referring again to the analogy of Jesus writing a higher decree to nullify the decree of sin against us and the enemy who desires to enforce it, we read, ***"... that through death He might destroy him who had the power of death, that is the devil, and release those who through fear of death were all their lifetime subject to bondage,"*** ~Hebrews 2:14-15. Do we not see this so perfectly pictured in our parable?

Your Will, Not Mine

Note, too, in our parable, that while Mordecai writes the new decree of what will take place, he can do nothing without Ahasuerus granting his approval. We sometimes give verbal assent to God's will in our life, but we hold back our veto power - just in case we don't like the direction God is taking us. We guard the things we are not ready to relinquish. We need to say with Ahasuerus, "As you please" – humbling ourselves in childlike submission to the will of our heavenly Father. As also Jesus taught us to pray, *"YOUR will be done, in earth (in me) as it is in heaven."* ~ Matthew 6:9. And as Jesus Himself prayed, *"nevertheless, not my will, but Yours be done!"*~Luke 22:42.

Permission to Take Plunder

An interesting detail regarding the battle that we don't want to miss, is in the instructions that Mordecai wrote into his decree on how the battle was to be fought. He orders that the Jews kill everything - everything that is against them, whether it looks innocent, or not, *("be it little children or women")*. Then he adds this permissive footnote – they are allowed to take plunder.

We will be looking at this again a little later, so for now let it suffice to understand that taking plunder can be a good thing, even though it is the spoils of a battle.

This can have a rather interesting application for our 'inner life'. We are never to allow anything in the flesh to have power over us - but we can use whatever is available to us, for the good of our kingdom. For example, when the love of food becomes an addiction, that power must be annihilated, but food may remain as something we use for sustenance and pleasure. We do not have to restrict ourselves to a bland or boring diet. Love of money must be radically 'killed' in our kingdom, but we can use the plunder of resources to serve us and be a blessing. Laziness must be destroyed, but the plunder of quiet meditation is something good. God did not design that we should live a self-depreciating, or masochistic lifestyle, but rather that we learn to live in joyful contentment under His abundant blessings, as Paul gave direction to Timothy, ***"Command those who are rich in this present age not to be haughty, nor to trust in uncertain riches but in the living God, who gives us richly all things to enjoy!"*** ~I Timothy 6:17.

(In a wider interpretation than what is covered in this book which is limited to our inner life we can take the plunder analogy to also include how we relate to the things of the world. If something of the world has power over us to draw us away from the Lord, then we need to ***"cut it off"***, but if we can use it for the kingdom then we can freely partake as we wish. The best plunder we can take from the world is sinners - the fruit of our evangelizing being the plunder of souls taken out of the world and brought into the kingdom on God.)

CHAPTER TWENTY-THREE

Joy!

Esther 8:15-17

Meantime the decree had been given out in the royal palace at Susa; 15and Mordecai had gone out from the presence of the king in royal garments of violet and white and with a great crown of gold and with a robe of fine linen and purple. The people of Susa shouted and were glad. 16To the Jews there came light and gladness and joy and honor. 17And in every province and city, wherever the king's command and decree came, there was gladness and joy among the Jews and a holiday. Many of the peoples of the earth professed to be Jews, for fear of the Jews took possession of them.

Good news! How we love it! Have you noticed that if you receive the kind of good news that fills you with joy, the first thing you want to do is share it with someone? Joy never wants to celebrate alone. When I was a child, I loved the acrostic I learned for the word JOY -partly because Joy is my middle name. But I loved how the secret to having 'joy' was hidden in the acrostic, Jesus first - Others next - Yourself last. When we have the order right in ourselves - in our thoughts, our attitudes, our actions - the fountain of joy bubbles up from deep within and overflows.

The best news of all is the word of God and what He has done for us. Psalm 96:2 declares, ***"Sing to the Lord, bless His name, proclaim the good news of His salvation from day to day."*** Everything changes when we have the promise of something good to come, especially when disaster is averted. Everything in us is affected by good news - we are full of ***"light and gladness and joy and honor"!*** We want to celebrate.

Even though the reality of the promise is not yet theirs, the people of Esther rejoice believing the promise to be true! Do we rejoice in faith having ***"the evidence of what*** (is***) yet unseen,"*** ~ Hebrews 11:1? How many promises of God's goodness do we have that cover every need we could possibly have - even if we do not yet see, or hold, the tangible answer to our need? As a believer we have no reason NOT to be filled with joy ... from moment to moment, from day to day! "The check IS in the mail!"

Imagine that every Christ-follower would be known for their inner joy; that a believer could be identified because their face shone with joy, their words were filled with joy, their actions and expressions one to another were full of joy! Would our world not be a different place? How sad that we claim the ***"joy of the Lord as our strength,"*** but then we hide it under a bushel. (Nehemiah 8:10)

CHAPTER TWENTY-FOUR

Never too Late

Esther 9:1

Now in the twelfth month (that is the month of Adar), on the thirteenth day, when the king's command and his decree was about to put into execution, on the day that the enemies of the Jews hoped to gain the mastery over them, then the tables were turned so that the Jews had the mastery over those who hated them

As we have already noted, Mordecai's decree is dated for the same day that Haman's revenge against the Jews is in readiness to be carried out. We order our lives paying attention to the 'right timing' and we know that God too gives careful attention to timing. Galatians 4:4 gives us an example, *"But when the fullness of the time had come, God sent forth His son..."* God's delay as He waits for that perfect time to send the answer to our prayer often makes us anxious, and when we reach the point of despair, fearing God will come too late, then suddenly we see Him act. It has been said that God is never late, but seldom is He early. God waits for several reasons. One - because He waits until all the pieces for His deliverance, or answers are in place. Two - in the waiting we learn patience. Three - when we see God come through for us, even at the twelfth hour, our trust in Him is strengthened and the next time we face trouble, our anxiety is held at bay because we remember that God was faithful last time, though it looked impossible. Four – God loves His work to be center-stage so that there is no doubt about who performed it.

Esther 9:2-17

The Jews gathered together in the cities throughout all the provinces of King Ahasuerus, to attack anyone who tried to harm them. No one could withstand them, for the fear of them had fallen on all the peoples. 3All the princes of the provinces and the satraps and the governors and they who attended to the king's business, helped the Jews, because the fear of Mordecai had fallen on them. 4For Mordecai was great in the king's palace, and as his power increased his fame spread throughout all the provinces. 5The Jews put all their enemies to the sword and, with slaughter and destruction, they did what they wanted to those who hated them. 6In Susa the capital the Jews killed five hundred people. 7They killed Parshandatha, Dalphon, Aspatha, 8Poratha, Adalia, Aridatha, 9Parmashta, Arisia, Aridai, and Vaizatha, 10the ten sons of Haman the son of Hammedatha, the Jews' enemy; but they did not take any plunder. 11On that day the number of those who were slain in Susa was brought before the king, 12and the king said to Queen Esther, "The Jews have slain five hundred people in Susa, and the ten sons of Haman. What then have they done in the rest of the king's provinces! Now what is your petition? It will be granted to you. What is your request? It will be done." 13Then Esther said, "If it please the king, let it be granted to the Jews who are in Susa to do tomorrow also according to this day's decree. Let the bodies of Haman's ten sons be hanged on the gallows." 14And the king commanded it to be done. A decree was given out in Susa and they hung the bodies of Haman's ten sons on the gallows. 15The Jews who were in Susa gathered themselves together again on the fourteenth day of the month of Adar. They killed three hundred people in Susa. But they did not take any plunder. 16And the other Jews who were in the king's provinces gathered themselves together and fought for their lives and overcame their enemies. They killed seventy-five thousand who hated them. But they did not take any plunder. 17This was on the thirteenth day of Adar.

When Mordecai's people come against their enemies, we find it interesting to see that there is no resistance at all against them. This is such a neat picture of the things of the flesh not having a backbone to stand against us when we 'decree' that the things of God will rule in our life.

Mordecai is rising in importance in relationship to Ahasuerus. He has become great "in the King's palace" – no longer sitting at the gate, no longer ignored - he is close to the king. We are told his power and fame is increasing, and his influence is spreading throughout the kingdom. Is that not what should be happening in every believer's life? The power, and fame, and influence of God's Spirit in our life, taking on the reality of more and more of Him and less and less of ourselves? John the Baptist speaks of this, in John 3:30, where he says, ***"He must increase, but I must decrease."***

The Power of Unity

The day the Jews in our parable had feared has come, but how contrary to their fears does it play out! We see the Jews are of one mind. What power there is in unity of mind and purpose! There is a oneness of resolve and diligence to fulfill all that is needful. Note that there is no indication of any resistance - in fact the 'enemy' is cowering in fear, knowing there is nothing they can do to save themselves. Our 'will' is a fearsome thing … it has more power than we give it credit for. Here, too, we are created in the image of God. His will cannot be countered, and neither can our will in ruling over our own kingdom. Notice, also, their weapon of choice - the sword. Does that not ring scripture bells? When we are admonished to take up the armor of our warfare, the word of God is symbolized by the sword. If we have God's word in our heart, in our mind, and in our mouth - knowing it, believing it and acting on it - there is no enemy that can stand against us. The voice of the flesh will become dim, and the things of the flesh will cower before the power of our will to deny them expression.

The Sons of Haman

We heaved a sigh of relief when Haman was finally hanged, and we expected the kingdom to be at peace. But, now, we see that this is not so. We have looked at the parallel between putting Haman to death and crucifying the flesh. We 'hanged Haman' when we turned from serving the flesh and resolved to serve God with an obedient heart. We think the battle is won, but then to our surprise, we find that we still struggle. While we have dealt with the big problem, there is still an ongoing dilemma - Haman is dead, but his sons are still alive and they too must be killed. So, then, what do the 'sons of Haman' represent? They are the characteristics, or sins, of the flesh that we struggle against daily

What we are dealing with is a little like a garden. We look with dismay at our garden plot, after we have been away for a couple of weeks, seeing that the weeds are choking out the harvest we are expecting to receive. We tackle the job and pull out every weed by the roots. Relieved, we admire the neat, clean rows of good plants that promise to yield a healthy crop. Can we now walk away until it is harvest time? No, we can't, because we know that we need to stay on top of it, pulling out the weeds as they, again and again, dare to push up from the ground. It takes continuing diligence to keep a garden free from weeds.

So we, also, must stay diligent, dealing with the 'sons' of the flesh as we see them rearing up within us. They are the characteristics of the flesh that we struggle with daily – those sinful reactions that catch us off guard. We see this continuing battle portrayed in our parable. The sons were killed in verse 6, but then we see Esther ask Ahasuerus to do it again the next day according to the decree - and hang the sons of Haman. Sometimes, we find the thoughts, and attitudes, and sins we struggle against don't easily 'stay dead', and we have to deal with them over and over again. It is never a 'once-for-all' clean-up job in our life when we are dealing with the 'sons of Haman'. We must stay vigilant, "cleansing a spot on our garment" as soon as it appears, pulling up a sin-weed as soon as we notice it growing in our kingdom - even if we have to hang a 'son of Haman' again!

Identifying the Sons of Haman

We have ten sons of Haman identified by name, and we have learned that the meaning of names is important.

If you are not yet convinced that Esther has parable value, I think looking at the names of Haman's sons, will slay your last doubts. Haman symbolizes the flesh, so what would you expect from the 'sons' but characteristics of the flesh? It is quite amazing what the Persian meanings of the names reveal. As we look at the names of these sons, note how each meaning has to do with 'self'. If there is one thing that characterizes the flesh, is it not a focus on 'self'?

Parmashta - means 'pre-eminent self, or self-important'. This is the character trait that drives one to seek personal glory and accolades, wanting the center stage and to be continually praised and admired.

Parshandatha - means 'curious self'. This is not the character trait of a child seeking to explore and learn. No, this is the trait that motivates to pry into other people's business, becoming the gossiper eager to stir up slander against another.

Dalphon - means 'crafty, weeping self, given to self-pity'. This is the compassionate trait turned inward, being overly sensitive to anything that could be perceived as hurtful to 'self', often what we call a victim mentality.

Aspatha - means 'to heap together for self or self-sufficient'. This character trait continually looks out for number one ... greedy.

Poratha - means 'spend-thriftiness, generous only to self, selfish, self-indulgent'. This character trait is the hoarding, never denying oneself any pleasure.

Adalia - means 'self-justified'. This is the character trait that shows in always being right, trusting in self-wisdom, boasting even of being humble, never taking ownership of any wrongs.

Aridatha - means 'strong self'. This trait is never hesitating to push personal agenda, forcing their will upon others.

Arisai - means 'bold-self'. This is the trait that is insensitive to others, rude, loud, disrespectful, impudent, always having an opinion and butting into conversations.

Aridai - means 'self-dignified, proud, pride in self'. This trait takes pride in who they are, what they have accomplished.

Vajezatha - means 'pure self, self-righteous'. This trait considers itself so much better than someone else, ignoring the beam in their own eyes, to point out the mote in their brother's eye.

Considering the above sons of Haman and their meaning, is it not obvious that our sins are always involved with 'self' in some way? We recognize in the symbolism of our parable the importance of *"putting off"* the flesh, as we see in Colossians 3:5-9, *"Therefore put to death your members which are on the earth; fornication, uncleanness, passion, evil desire, and covetousness, which is idolatry, because of these things the wrath of God is coming upon the sons of disobedience ... but now you must also put off all these; anger wrath, malice, blasphemy, filthy language out of your mouth. Do not lie to one another, since you have put off the old man with all his deeds and have put on the new man who is renewed in knowledge according to the image of Him who created him."*

Did you notice in the just quoted passage how there is the *"putting to death"* ... and then the second, *"now you must also put off all these"?* We first crucify the flesh when we recognize that it is against us and we choose to make Jesus our Lord, but then we still struggle with the expression of fleshly characteristics in our life - a perfect parallel to the picture we see in the hanging of Haman and then the secondary killing and hanging of his sons.

Our parable picture presents a very ruthless dealing with the weaknesses of the flesh, there can be no compromise, no passive indifference, no shrugging of the shoulders. Looking again at, II Corinthians 10:3-6, brings this whole concept into sharp focus. *"For though we walk in the flesh, we do not war according to the flesh, for the weapons of our warfare are not carnal but mighty in God for pulling down strongholds, casting down arguments and every high thing that exalts itself against the knowledge of God, bringing every thought into captivity to the obedience of Christ, and being ready to punish all disobedience when your obedience is fulfilled."*

The above passage shows where the battle is fought and won – *"bringing every thought into captivity"*. The battleground is in our mind, where the sons of Haman lurk. If we take captive every errant, sinful thought as soon as it enters our mind, we will walk in victory. So here again, we see confirmation of Dr. Leaf's study, how important it is to 'rule' first over our thoughts, not allowing a negative or ungodly thought to take control of what follows in our kingdom.

When we, beginning with our thoughts, bring everything into submission to the Lord, we will become more and more 'like Christ' - being transformed into His image. Not only will our own kingdom become light, but our light will shine brighter in the dark world around us.

CHAPTER TWENTY-FIVE

Hang Them and Forget the Plunder!

Esther 9:10, 15, 16

"...but they did not lay a hand on the plunder."
"...but they did not lay a hand on the plunder."
"...but they did not lay a hand on the plunder."

There is a literary tool in Hebrew that when something is especially important it is repeated. Three times we have a repeated phrase here in this part of the parable, ***"but they did not lay a hand on the plunder."***

Even though Mordecai had given permission for plunder to be taken, we see that none was taken. Perhaps the people were so determined to wipe out all remnants of this evil planned against them, that they abhorred the very thought of taking any plunder. There is good reason for us to stop and reflect on the significance of this repeated phrase. If it was noted only once, we would probably skim over it without recognizing the intended interpretation that pertains to us, but three repeats should grab our attention.

God's Battle Instructions Regarding Plunder

To understand something more about taking plunder in a battle, we need to go back again to the original instructions God gave the Israelites. In Deuteronomy 20, God commanded Israel that if in their travels they encountered a city that refused their extended hand of peace, they were to kill every male in the city with the sword. But afterwards, they were allowed to take plunder - as we read in Deuteronomy 20:14, ***"But the women, the little ones, the livestock, and all that is in the city, all its spoil, you shall plunder for yourself; and you shall eat the enemies' plunder which the Lord your God gives you."***

There is a key in God's instructions that has meaning for us today. Why kill all the males? The males represented the strength of the city, the power to take up arms against God's people. With the males dead, Israel was free to enjoy the plunder without any fear of harm. The plunder was good and useful to them. In Proverbs 13:22, we read that, ***"... the wealth of the sinner is stored up for the righteous."***

We see the same pattern in the parable of Esther. Mordecai, in Esther 8:11, instructs the Jews to ***"destroy, kill, and annihilate all the forces of any people or province that would assault them both little children*** *and women...*" and then he gives them permission to plunder their possessions. Again, with the power of the enemy destroyed, their possessions posed no threat.

What are we meant to understand from the fact that even though Mordecai gave permission for the Jews to take plunder, they did not take any at all?

Perhaps we can find a clue to the answer in Jesus' words that sound rather harsh to us. We referred to this passage earlier, but let us look at it again. In Matthew 18:8-9, He says, *"And if your hand or foot causes you to sin, cut it off and cast it from you. It is better for you to enter into life lame or maimed, rather than having two hands or two feet, to be cast into the everlasting fire. And if your eye causes you to sin, pluck it out and cast it from you...."*

Are our hands, and feet, and eyes good things to have? Meant to be fully enjoyed and useful to us? Yes, of course, but when are we to cast them from us? When they cause us to sin. Here is the key to when plunder is good and when it is best that *"we do not lay our hand on the plunder."* We are all different in what we can control and what so easily takes control of us. The question we must continually ask ourselves is, "Is this thing I allow myself to have, hindering me in seeking a closer walk with the Lord? Does it cause me to be tempted to turn aside, to entertain ungodly thoughts or emotions or actions?"

We have Paul as our example regarding 'plunder'. In I Corinthians 6:12, he says, *"All things are lawful for me but all things are not helpful. All things are lawful for me but I will not be brought under the power of any."*

And again in I Corinthians 10:23, he says, *"All things are lawful for me but all things are not helpful, all things are lawful for me, but all things do not edify."* Just as the parable repeats this detail, so the interpretation is also repeated.

Rather than risk a compromise, even if it is allowable for someone else, we need to stay away from anything that might cause us to sin. Better we declare, **"I will not lay my hand on the plunder."**

CHAPTER TWENTY-SIX

Finally, the Good Life

Esther 9:18-19

On the fourteenth day of the month Adar the Jews rested and made it a day of feasting and rejoicing. 18(But the Jews in Susa gathered on both the thirteenth and fourteenth day --- and rested on the fifteenth day of the same month and made it a day of feasting and rejoicing.) 19This is why the Jews who live in the country villages keep the fourteenth day of the month of Adar as a day of rejoicing and feasting and a holiday, and a day in which they send gifts of food to each other.

It is wonderful to read of the kingdom in holiday mode, celebrating with feasting and rejoicing! All through the ages we have celebrated with feasting. We can't even imagine a 'get together', for any reason, without food - be it a birthday, a wedding, a housewarming or a holiday. While we need food for life, we make food much more than that; we eat because we enjoy it. This pleasure will continue in eternity as we look forward to the Lamb's wedding supper – the ultimate in banquet celebration! It was food that caused our death in the Garden of Eden, but it is also food that gives us life, both physical and spiritual.

God desires His children to rejoice and celebrate His goodness. When our 'kingdom' is in order and we have made God our delight, we have so much to celebrate! We feast on His Word, we drink the water of life, we praise Him with song and dance, and express the generosity of our overflowing heart.

Esther 9:20-22

Mordecai had these things recorded. He sent letters to all the Jews who were in all the provinces of the King Ahasuerus, both near and far. 21He told them to keep the fourteenth day of the month of Adar and also the fifteenth day every year, 22as the days on which the Jews had rest from their enemies, and the month which was turned from sorrow to gladness and from mourning into a feast day. They should make them days of feasting and gladness and of sending gifts of food to each other and of gifts to the poor.

Holidays are built on tradition and are for the purpose of remembering a memorable event we do not want to forget. Along with feasting and gladness, Ahasuerus' kingdom sent gifts to one another and did not forget the poor. Sounds like Christmas, doesn't it? And what is worth celebrating more than freedom? *"Therefore, if the Son shall make you free, you shall be free indeed!"* ~

John 8:36. We are free! No evil, no enemy can destroy us. For all eternity we are free!

Let the celebrating never end!

Esther 9:23-32

So what the Jews had begun to do they adopted as a custom, just as Mordecai had written to them. 24For Haman the son of Hammedatha, the Agagite, the enemy of all the Jews, had plotted to destroy them. He had cast 'Pur', that is the lot, intending to consume them and to destroy them. 25But when the matter came before the king, he gave written orders that his wicked plot, which he had planned against the Jews, should come upon his own head, and that he and his sons should be hanged on the gallows. 26This is why these days are called Purim, after the word Pur. Therefore because of all the words of this letter, as well as all they had seen, and all they had experienced, 27the Jews established and made it a custom for them, for their descendants, and for all who should join them, so that it might not be repealed, that they should continue to observe these two days as feasts each year, 28and that these days should be remembered and kept throughout every generation, every family, every province, and every city. And these days of Purim should not pass away from among the Jews nor the remembrance of them disappear among their descendants. 29Queen Esther, the daughter of Abihail, gave Mordecai the Jew all authority in writing to confirm this second letter of Purim. 30He sent letters to all the Jews, to the hundred and twenty-seven provinces of the kingdom of Ahasuerus, wishing them peace and security, 31to confirm these days of Purim in their proper times, to be observed as Mordecai the Jew and Queen Esther had directed and as the Jews had prescribed for themselves and their descendants, in the matter of the fastings and their cry of lamentation. 32And the commands of Esther confirmed these matters of Purim; and it was written in the records.

In this part of the parable we have references to Haman with words like, plotted, intended, planned - but all his works were turned to naught. Our flesh is a powerful enemy, but in the believer who is strong in the Lord, the sins and weaknesses of the flesh have been 'put off', and the 'new character' has been 'put on'. *"Therefore, as the elect of God, holy and beloved, put on tender mercies, kindness, humbleness of mind, meekness, long suffering....But above all these things put on love, which is the bond of perfection,"* ~Colossians 3:12,14. *"But put on the Lord Jesus Christ, and make no provision for the flesh, to fulfill its lusts,"* ~Romans 12:14.

Keeping Traditions

We also see that, in our parable story, traditions were set in place that have been kept, and celebrated, each year - even up to our present time! We love traditions, they keep us centered and bring family and friends together. When there is a momentous event or milestone, we want to create some tradition around it so that we do not forget it, and in celebrating it each year we experience again the joy of the event. The celebrating also provides an opportunity to share with others the good things we have received. We pass on the traditions to our children and children's children creating memories for them that shape their lives.

But to stay true to our parable interpretation, the analogy to the celebrated traditions is that we develop habits that will help us to remember the things we have received of the Lord, the lessons we have learned, and the experiences we want to remember. Traditions, or habits such as - listening to worship music, having a daily quiet time, spending time in prayer, studying and memorizing God's Word, rejoicing in thanksgiving, keeping a journal – are all examples of personal 'traditions' that keep us returning again and again to the joy of our salvation, abiding in and enjoying the One who redeemed us and set us free.

Esther 10:1-3

King Ahasuerus imposed a tribute on the land and the coasts. 2All the acts of his power and of his might, and the full account of the greatness of Mordecai to which the king advanced him, are they not recorded in the book of the chronicles of the kings of Media and Persia? 3 For Mordecai the Jew was next in rank to King Ahasuerus, and great among the Jews, and

loved by them all. He sought the good of his people and promoted the welfare of their descendants.

Ahasuerus imposes a tribute on his kingdom. He remains in control of his kingdom and demands that everyone pay what he demands. That sounds like his kingdom rule is going backwards! But wait - the Hebrew word translated 'tribute' has the meaning of burden. So then we could glean from this symbolism that we must rule over our 'kingdom' is such a way that every part of our kingdom contributes to the work and purpose to which we are called. I think of the verse in Galatians 6:5 that says, **"For each one must bear his own load."** Or as some translations say, **"his own burden".** Stretching this verse to fit our parable interpretation, we could say that our whole body must participate in what our 'will' chooses to do. Our mouth, in what it says, must pay tribute to our 'will'; our ears must pay tribute in what they listen to; our hands must pay tribute in the work they find to do; and our feet must pay tribute for where they go. So as our will has determined to follow the Holy Spirit, the will must make sure that the whole kingdom - body, soul, and spirit'- prospers in the things of the Lord. **"Now may the God of peace Himself sanctify your whole spirit, soul and body be preserved blameless at the coming of our Lord Jesus Christ."** ~ I Thessalonians 5:23

O Give Thanks and Acknowledge Him!

We read in our parable, that everything was recorded, even as we record everything in our memory. I think of Psalm 107 that four times repeats God's expressed longing, ***"Oh that men would give thanks to the Lord for His goodness and for His wonderful works to the children of men!"*** Is our parable not encouraging us to record and remember all the acts of goodness that God has done for us and all the wonderful words He has spoken ... and that we should think on them often? Should our life not be a life of thanksgiving for all the things God has done? Dietrich Bonhoeffer said, "Gratitude changes the pangs of memory into a tranquil joy!"

I always feel a deep sense of pleasure when secular studies or scientific discoveries come to conclusions that support what God recorded in scripture thousands of years ago. Dr. Robert Emmons is the world's leading scientific expert on gratitude, well known for his over a decade study and his books on the subject. His studies have shown, over and over again, how an attitude of gratitude leads to a fuller, healthier, and happier life. One of Emmons' studies involved college students with debilitating physical illnesses. To his surprise these people, who had the most to complain about, had the greatest sense of gratitude for the things in their life they were thankful for. He drew three conclusions from this study.

1. Gratitude can be an overwhelming intense feeling.

2. Gratitude for gifts that others easily overlook can be the most powerful and frequent form of thankfulness.

3. Gratitude can be chosen in spite of one's situation or circumstances.

Why does scripture repeatedly admonish us to be thankful and express our gratitude to God? Because it is what gives us the 'good life' no matter what goes on around us. Our Heavenly Father desires us to live in joy and blessing, and a thankful attitude is the key to unlock the good life!

Abiding in Him

At the end of our parable, we see Mordecai next in rank to King Ahasuerus ... and he is greatly loved. He seeks the good of his people and peace in his kingdom. We do not need to elaborate the parable meaning here. Do we not love God when we live in His presence? Are we not overwhelmed by His goodness when we see His care of us? Is He not our Prince of Peace whose peace passes all understanding? Is His indwelling Spirit not our help and comfort?

But to bask in this abiding place of goodness, we must not forget that as great as the Holy Spirit is in our lives, as much as we exalt him and love him ... the Spirit of God is always subject to our will. Only as we allow him to rule in our lives does he rule. Our free will is never violated. It is hard to believe that the authority of our will is so supreme that even God will not overrule it. We see this truth portrayed in the story of Jesus walking on the water. Obviously, Jesus wanted to go to his disciples; He saw them struggling against the storm, yet, in Mark 6:48, we see that He *"would have passed them by."* Not until they cried out to Him, did He go to them. How often do we let Jesus pass us by because we do not 'will' that He should come to us? It is the greatest gift we can give God when we yield ourselves to Him, make His Word our law, and place our submissive trust in Him, declaring that *"in all our ways we WILL acknowledge Him,"* ~Proverbs 3:6. In Him, we truly find the good life!

And so ends the parable of Esther. May we remember what we have seen in the mirror and what we have learned from studying our own reflection in it.

In Conclusion - For Such a Time

This parable interpretation of the story of Esther could be said to be heavy on the negative since so much attention is on the sins of the flesh. But, as Mordecai's famous words state, *"For such a time as this,"* I am wondering if today is "such a time" when we need to be reminded of the deceptive power of the flesh. I am daily shocked to see how different the world is from how I experienced it in the years of my childhood and youth. More and more, the church – going along with the world – is taking a compromising attitude to the word of God, replacing the literal understanding of scripture with a more palatable interpretation. It is not possible to move away from the things of God without moving toward the things of the flesh.

We have a description of the sins and attitudes of

people living in the last days, *"But know this, that in the last days perilous times will come; for men will be lovers of themselves, lovers of money, boasters, proud, blasphemers, disobedient to parents, unthankful, unholy, unloving, unforgiving, slanderers, without self-control, brutal, despisers of good, having a form of godliness but denying its power. And from such people turn away,"* ~II Timothy 3:1-5.

The above list is apropos, as anyone living in today's world would have to admit. Having just studied Haman and his sons, we understand who *"the people"* are that we are to turn away from. But what is the answer? How are we then, as victorious believers, to live in today's world? While Paul, in the above passage, aptly describes prevailing attitudes of the end time, Jesus gives us a commandment as well. We read His words in Luke 21:28, where He speaks about the days that will precede His coming, *"Now when these things begin to happen, look up and lift up your heads, because your redemption draws near."* The Greek word that is translated 'lift up your heads' is 'elated'. Jesus is saying that the response He is looking for from those who are living in end times is an attitude of joy! How can we do that? Is that not an ostrich reaction? No, Jesus is not saying that we are to be ignorant of what is around us, but to keep our eyes on Him. We look up to Him knowing that, in Him, we have everything we need. We know the best is yet to come and is about to begin! Our redemption is not just for this life but for all eternity!

There are two attitudes that effectively cripple the

power of the things of the flesh and the world that threaten us. These attitudes are joy and thankfulness. Philippians 4:4 says, ***"Rejoice in the Lord ALWAYS and again I will say, rejoice!"*** And in I Thessalonians 5:18, we read, ***"In everything give thanks, for this is the will of God in Christ Jesus for you."*** The parable of Esther ends with the people filled with thanksgiving and great joy! No matter what happens, if we look up with great joy for what God has purposed for us, and if we are full of thanksgiving for who He is and who we are in Him, how can we not walk in victory, experiencing all the 'good life' that is in Him and is ours to enjoy for today and all eternity

> ***"Now may the God of hope, fill you with all joy and peace in believing, that you may abound in hope by the power of the Holy Spirit."*** -Romans 15:13.

QUICK REFERENCE CHART

The Mirror	The Reflection
CHAPTER ONE	
Ahasuerus - a title, not a name, for the King	Our will – the throne from where we rule our kingdom
Ahasuerus' love of feasting and partying – seeking the good life	The Me-Myself-and- I lifestyle, where we live to please ourselves
Shushan or citadel – Ahasuerus never leaves it	Our physical body, that we never leave throughout our earthly life
Ahasuerus' kingdom over which he rules	Our kingdom, over which we rule – body, soul, and spirit
Ahasuerus' palace – beautiful in splendor and whiteness	We are wonderfully created in the image of the glory of God – originally without sin and whiteness and can again be covered in Jesus' righteousness - 'white/pure'
CHAPTER TWO	
Vashti – the queen	Our spirit

Vashti refuses to obey king's command	We cannot command our spirit contrary to the purpose for which God gave it
Eunuchs who serve the king	The 'lifeless' justifying excuses we give to make ourselves comfortable in selfish desires or our sins of choice
CHAPTER THREE	
Ahasuerus is upset, humiliated and seeks counsel, advice	We are upset, when our plans go awry, and when we want someone to come alongside, we seek advice from sympathetic sources
Ahasuerus' seven wise men who give advice that feeds Ahasuerus' ego and his self-interest	We seek advice from the world that makes us feel good and supports us in what we want to do – confirming us – not recognizing that it will leave us empty and unfulfilled
Ahasuerus rules, doing as he pleases	We too are guilty – 'every man does that which is right in his own eyes' – in our carnality, we please ourselves
CHAPTER FOUR	
Time passes, Ahasuerus reconsiders, and feels regret for having rejected his queen	We impulsively act and react in the heat of the moment, but then time passes and we reconsider our decisions, recognizing that we have lost more than we have gained.

Ahasuerus feels regret, and loneliness, but he seeks his own solutions	We feel an emptiness, know we are missing something, but we try to fill that God-space within us with all the wrong things
CHAPTER FIVE	
Mordecai	The Holy Spirit of God
Esther	Our 'new spirit'
In all things, Esther is submissive to and obedient to Mordecai	Our spirit is what makes us spiritual beings able to communicate with God – through His Spirit to our spirit we hear His voice and sense His presence.
CHAPTER SIX	
Esther is chosen by Ahasuerus to be his queen	When we get ourselves a 'new spirit', we are born again – our new life begins
Ahasuerus full of joy, celebrates	Having received salvation and forgiveness, we feel the joy and peace that comes from the Lord – 'the grass is greener, the sky is bluer'
Ahasuerus continues to do what he did before	Though we are 'born again', the sanctification process has just begun, we do not immediately become 'holy'

CHAPTER SEVEN	
Virgins are gathered a second time	Though we are spiritually born again, we are yet carnal, one foot in the kingdom of God and one foot in the world
The Doorkeepers	Our eyes and our ears through which we receive information and knowledge
Putting the Doorkeepers to death	Putting 'to death' the desire to watch or listen to what we as believers should not watch or listen to - things that do not promote godly thoughts, attitudes or actions
CHAPTER EIGHT	
Haman	the flesh, our old nature that is contrary to the things of God
Enmity between Haman and Mordecai	The enmity between our flesh and our spirit
Ahasuerus exalts Haman	We allow the weaknesses of our flesh – the sins of our flesh - to have pre-eminence in our life, we choose the easy way rather than choosing to pursue godliness
CHAPTER NINE	
Haman casts the lot	Trusting in empty superstition

The day the lot falls on	God's providence as He watches over us to protect us from intended harm against us, giving us time to strengthen ourselves to stand against temptation or attack of the enemy
The people Haman warns Ahasuerus about that are dispersed throughout his kingdom	The things of God that have entered our heart and mind and have begun to change us
Ahasuerus refuses Haman's monetary enticement	We are not all tempted in the same way, by the same temptations - we all have areas of weakness where we give in to temptation, and areas where we are strong enough to resist
Haman's enticing words	Temptation always comes promising 'gain' and never reveals to us the resulting harm if we give in
Ahasuerus' signet ring	Symbolizes the authority of our will – nothing happens without our 'stamp' of approval

CHAPTER TEN	
A Persian decree could not be changed or revoked	Our thoughts cannot be 'unthought' - our thoughts begin a process of change throughout our 'kingdom' that cannot be revoked
Haman and Ahasuerus sit down to drink	We are naturally comfortable with our flesh, and satisfying the desires of our flesh make us feel 'good'
The kingdom was in turmoil	Though we relish the 'feel-good' emotions of satisfying our flesh, we are unaware of the damage/hurt that has already begun as a consequence of our sinful thought or actions
CHAPTER ELEVEN	
The grief of Mordecai	Pictures the grief of God when His child wanders from the truth
CHAPTER TWELVE	
Esther sends clothing to Mordecai	God does not need or want us to comfort Him, He wants us to repent and turn away from what He knows will hurt us

Ahasuerus ignoring Esther, as he keeps company with Haman	When we indulge the flesh, we pull away from the things of God, forget to spend time and fellowship with Him, and become weak, not having fed ourselves spiritually
Esther as the link between Mordecai and Ahasuerus	It is through our spirit that we have communication and fellowship with God – His Spirit communing with our spirit
CHAPTER THIRTEEN	
Entering the throne room without an invitation – penalty of death	We 'kill' any thought or advice or idea or information that we do not want – we allow into our mind only that we consent to – what we 'will' to think about
Esther is there "for such a time as this"	We too have a purpose that is unique to us, something we can do for the kingdom of God that no one else can do
Esther is guided by Mordecai – she is obedient to him in all things	The spirit of the believer is under submission to the Holy Spirit who guides and directs and informs.

CHAPTER FOURTEEN	
"Up to half of my kingdom"	Though we are called to wholeheartedly serve the Lord, He never takes 'possession' of us - we keep our free will and, only as we give assent, can God rule in our lives
CHAPTER FIFTEEN	
Esther banqueting with Haman and Ahasuerus	The more time we spend fellowshipping in the spirit, feeding on the things of God, the less we will desire the 'fellowship' or things of the flesh
Zeresh - Haman's wife	The flesh never delivers on its promises and Zeresh symbolizes the end result – misery and unfulfilled desire
The 75 foot gallows	The extreme we go to when we seek retribution for our wounded pride or humiliation or offence committed against us

CHAPTER SIXTEEN	
Ahasuerus reviewing life in his kingdom	We record the events of our life in our memory, and at night or in quiet times, we reflect and consider ... and oft we realize that we have left undone something that needs to be addressed, or in hindsight, we come to a place of appreciation and thankfulness for what the Lord has done for us – and our response is to praise Him, honor Him in some way
CHAPTER SEVENTEEN	
Ahasuerus consults Haman on how to reward and honor Mordecai	We instinctively know how to honor someone, because we know what we ourselves would want. When we recognize the goodness of the Lord, we no longer want to satisfy the desires of the flesh, but want in every way to exalt the Lord and His ways in our life
Haman's humiliation	When we are filled with praise and thanksgiving to the Lord, the flesh is humbled, and has no power to influence us

CHAPTER EIGHTEEN	
Ahasuerus is finally aware of Haman being his enemy	The more time we spend with the Lord, the clearer and deeper our insight, and we gain wisdom to discern what is of the Lord and what isn't
CHAPTER NINETEEN	
No communication between Esther and Haman	Our spirit has no fellowship with the flesh – and it is in our will that we determine who we will keep company with
Ahasuerus' anger against Haman	It is a sign of maturity when we react with righteous anger against sin – against anything that exalts itself contrary to God
Haman hanged	Crucifying of the flesh – putting to death its power over us
CHAPTER TWENTY	
Mordecai in the palace	When we crucify the flesh with its desires, we make room for the Holy Spirit to take a prominent and intimate place in our life

CHAPTER TWENTY-ONE	
Haman is dead but the decree still stands	We all deserve God's condemnation against us because we have all sinned and come short of the glory of God – that decree cannot be changed
The New Decree – written by Mordecai, instead of Ahasuerus	We have no idea how to undo our messes or find a solution for our sin stained soul - it is wisdom on our part to give it all to the Lord, and trust in His mercy
CHAPTER TWENTY-TWO	
A decree that over rules the old one, without revoking it	God brought in a New Covenant that overruled the decree against us – Jesus' death in our place set us free from all condemnation and offered forgiveness from all sin – offers life instead of death
Mordecai orders a massacre	The ruthlessness with which we deal with the sins or weaknesses of our flesh

Permission to take plunder	We must not allow anything to rule over us that would tempt us away from the things of God, but we can use anything for good in our life
CHAPTER TWENTY-THREE	
Joy in the Kingdom at the announcement of the new decree	We have a 'book' full of the promises of God, some fulfilled, some for today, and some for the future – but all them are cause for rejoicing because we can put our trust in them knowing that there is nothing that can come between us and God's love for us and His care over us
CHAPTER TWENTY-FOUR	
The sons of Haman	The characteristics of the flesh – the attitudes and habits that we need to continually guard against – our spiritual battle

CHAPTER TWENTY-FIVE	
They did not lay hands on the plunder	As Paul recognized in his own life and also taught that while all things are lawful, even good things may not always edify and so sometimes it is better to avoid them rather than compromise our faith in some way
CHAPTER TWENTY-SIX	
Joy, thanksgiving, traditions	Abiding in the Lord is where the good life is, and building good habits in our life to continually remind us of what is important, of what the Lord has done, and who He is in our life, that we will not forget, but walk in joy and thanksgiving.

BIBLIOGRAPHY

Introduction

a) In the third year of his reign King Xerxes (486-465), the Great King, The king of Persia is King Ahasuerus in the book of Esther – for a full discussion of his life, see Yamauchi 1990;203-205,226-239

b) Little is known about the last years of Xerxes' life. After his reversal in Greece, he withdrew into himself and allowed himself to be drawn into harem intrigues in which he was, in fact, only a pawn; thus, he disposed of his brother's entire family at the demand of the queen. But in 465 BCE he himself fell, together with his eldest son, under the blows of murderous members of his court, among them his minister Artabanus. Another son, Artaxerxes I, succeeded in retaining power. Jean-Louis Huot, Encyclopedia Britannica

c) Despite the fact that both Josephus ("Ant."xi 6) and the Septuagint refer to Ahasuerus as Artxerxes, modern scholars, such as Keil ("Commentary to Esther"), Bertheau, and Ryssel ("Commentary to

Esther") Wildeboer ("Jurzer Hand-Kommentar,"
1898), Sayce ("Higher Criticism and the
Monuments," p. 469) and Schrader ("K.A.T."
p375) are agreed that Xerxes and none other is
meant by Ahasuerus, and this for various reasons;
(1) Ahasuerus is the attempt of the Hebrew to
represent the Persian Khshayarsh, the aleph
being prosthetic just as it is in Ahashdarpenim
(Esth.iii.12) where the Persian is Kschatrapawan
(Wildeboer, *in loco*) The Greek represents it by
Xerxes. (2) The description that Herodotus gives
of the character of Xerxes corresponds to the
Biblical and, later, the midrashic picture –vain,
foolish, fickle, and hot-tempered. (3) The king
must be a Persian, for the whole atmosphere is
Persian. The court is at Shushan and the officers
are Persian. (4) Between the third and seventh
years of his reign Ahasuerus is lost to view in
the Biblical account' but that was just the time
when Xerxes was engaged in the invasion of
Greece. There can therefore be no doubt that the
monarch whose name passed among the Hebrews
as Ahasuerus was the one known as Khshayarsha
in the Persain inscriptions and among the Greeks
as Xerxes. Quote from – Ahasuerus, by Gerson
B. Levi, Kaufmann Kihler, George A. Barton –
Jewish Encyclopedia, 1906

Chapter one

a) A study of Persian records indicates that Xerxes

(Achashveroshi) was a far more successful ruler than Herodotus would suggest ... Xerxes (Achashveroshi) used the fabulous wealth of his empire to build the most magnificent structure of Achaemonian times, the palace of Persepolis ... He did, of course, also build at Susa (Shushan) but that site is not well preserved today ... Xerxes' (Achashveroshi's) empire did expend from India to Ethiopia, and Xerxes (Achashveroshi) did have a winter palace at Susa (Shushan), which had features not incompatible with the architectural detail given in (the book of Esther). Famous for his lavish drinking parties and his extravagant promises and gifts, Xerxes (Achashveroshi) also had, on occasion, a nasty, irrational temper. (C. Moore, *Anchor Bible; Esther*, pp.XXXVIII-XLI)

b) "In the third year of his reign (1:3), Ahasuerus had a 'Pep Rally Party" to entice the various kings in his empire to join him on a military expedition to Greece. (Esther 1:3-22) At this lavish banquet, each participant got their own gold vessels (1:7) Each vessel was individually hand crafted and different from any other. This banquet was designed to encourage these kings to 'sign up for a Greek vacation' with their armies! One of my favorite objects in the Metropolitan Museum of Art in New York City is a gold drinking vessel that was bought on the antiquities market in Iran, allegedly near Susa. It is a beautifully stylized drinking cup with the front part of a lion on it, contemporary with this

banquet (Pittman 1987;140-141 ; plate 102) –
Gordon Franz MA (Thermopylae and the Book
of Esther – Associates for Biblical Research)

Chapter Two

a) **Vashti, the queen**. The only wife of Xerxes
known to the Greeks was Amestris, the daughter
of Otanes, one of the seven conspirators (Herod;
7.61). Xerxes probably took her to wife as soon
as he was of marriageable age, and before he
ascended the throne had a son by her, who in
his seventh year was grown up (*ibid.* 9.108).
It would seem to be certain that if Ahasuerus
is Xerxes, Vashti must be Amestris. The names
themselves are not very remote, since will readily
interchange with *v*; but Vashti might possibly
represent not the real name of the queen, but a
favourite epithet, such as *vahista,* "*sweetest.*"**Made
a feast for the women**. Men and women did not
take their meals together in Persia unless in the
privacy of domestic life. If the women, therefore,
were to partake in a festivity, it was necessary that
they should be entertained separately. In the royal
house. In the gynaeceum or harem, which was
probably on the southern side of the great pillared
hall at Susa (Fergusson). http://www.studylight.
org/commentaries/tpc/view.cgi?bk=es&ch=1

b) Again, no one shared the table of a Persian king
except his mother or his wedded wife, the wife
sitting below him, the mother above him; *The*

Parallel Lives – The Life of Artaxertes by Pultarch published in Vol. XI – 5-3

c) In 539 BC, the Persians conquered Mesopotamia and it became part of the Persian state. The veil and the seclusion of women were among the social habits that the Persians adopted from the Assyrians and maintained over the years. In ancient Persia, women of noble families became also secluded and had to be covered when they went out in public. – Alexandra Kinias – *History of the Veil- Part One, Veil in the Ancient World.*

d) It is also their general practice to deliberate upon affairs of weight when they are drunk; and then on the morrow, when they are sober, the decision to which they came the night before is put before them by the master of the house in which it was made; and if it is than approved of, they act on it, if not, they set it aside. Herodius I. 133

e) There is another peculiarity, which the Persians themselves have never noticed, but which has not escaped my observation. **Their names, which are expressive of some bodily or mental excellence,** all end with the same letter – the letter which is called San by the Dorians, and Sigma by the Ionians. Anyone who examines this will find that the Persian names, one and all without exception, end with this letter. Herodotus; *On the Customs of the Persians* I.139

MY MAIN SOURCES FOR NAME MEANINGS

Bible Study Tools – http://www.biblestudytools.com

The Bible Wheel - http://www.biblewheel.com/forumshowthread.php?762-Names-in-Esther-link-to-spoke-17

Mi Yodeya, http://www.judaism.stackexchange.com/ - Q&A site for those who base their lives on Jewish law and Tradition

Author contact - "I'd love to hear from you!"
Julie Klassen - <u>juliefrompearls@gmail.com</u>

Other books by this author
Adventures of Heart Longing
Heart Longing and the Treasure Keys

Printed in the United States
By Bookmasters